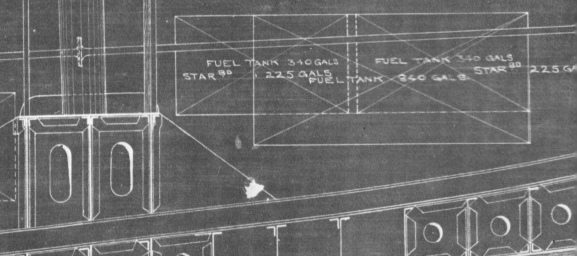

FUEL TANK 340 GALS

STAR BD 225 GALS

FUEL TANK 340 GALS

FUEL TANK 340 GALS STAR BD 225 GA

FUEL TANK 340 GALS STAR BD 225 GA

ANK

F. W. TANK

SALT-WATER PALACES

Endpapers
The endpapers show a facsimile of part of the accommodation plan of the 133 foot racing schooner MARGHERITA, *380 tons Thames measurement. The yacht was built in 1913 for Cecil Whitaker of Pylewell Park by Camper and Nicholson, to the designs of C.E. Nicholson.* MARGHERITA *was the last of the great Whitaker racing schooners that included the Fay designed* CICELY *of 263 tons Thames measurement, and the 352 ton* WATERWITCH, *whose masts, sails, rigging and cabin fittings were transferred to* MARGHERITA. (Camper & Nicholson)

SALT-WATER PALACES

Maldwin Drummond

Introduction by
Admiral of the Fleet The Earl Mountbatten of Burma

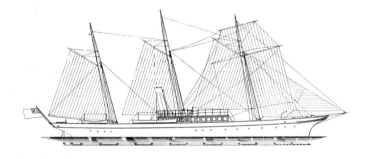

A Studio Book
THE VIKING PRESS·NEW YORK
in association with Debrett's Peerage Limited

To Gilly

Book designed by Roger Huggett and produced by Sinc
Phototypesetting by TNR Productions, London
Printed in the Netherlands by de Lange/van Leer BV

Illustrated on title page
The screw steam yacht FAIR GERALDINE R.Y.S., *designed and built by Ramage and
Ferguson at Leith, in 1880, for Lord Otho Fitzgerald. She was 148 feet overall and of
301 tons Thames measurement.* FAIR GERALDINE *was later known as* ONORA, AMELIA,
GERALDINE & VAZIFE. *Under this last name she did duty with the Turkish Customs.*

Frontispiece
NAMOUNA *in Venetian Waters by Julius Stewart, painted in 1890. The yacht, of 740
tons Thames measurement, was designed by the Master of the steam auxiliary, St.
Clare Byrne, for James Gordon Bennett Jr. and built by Ward Stanton & Co. of
Newburgh, N.Y., in 1882.*
*It is strange to see the afterguard forward. The view of Venice may have been better
from there or, more likely, the yacht was laid out below as his later vessel,* LYSISTRATA *of
2,089 tons Thames measurement, with the crew's quarters aft. This is perhaps the
finest picture ever painted of life aboard a large steam yacht in the 90's. (Wadsworth
Atheneum)*

Introduction

by

Admiral of the Fleet the Earl Mountbatten of Burma,

KG, PC, GCB, OM, GCSI, GCIE, GCVO, DSO, FRS

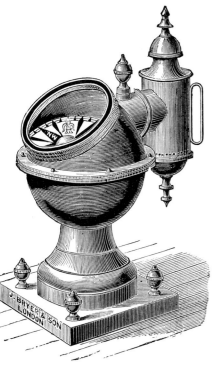

The joy of yachting was recognised as far back as the days of the Romans when the Roman lyric poet, Horace, wrote:

'They change their sky, not their soul,
who run across the sea.
We work hard at doing nothing;
we seek happiness in Yachts......'

But when King Charles II brought yachting to the Thames in 1660 even he could not have foreseen the enthusiasm for yachting that was to develop over the centuries.

The Royal Yacht was then and is now, with few exceptions, a Vessel of State and her presence has always invoked great interest. I well remember the great thrill of being taken on board the Royal Yacht, VICTORIA AND ALBERT, by my parents when I was a young boy and still feel the same sense of excitement whenever I have the honour to embark in the Royal Yacht BRITANNIA.

Some of the finest craftsmanship in Britain has been employed in building yachts, both large and small, not only for people in the United Kingdom, but for virtually every country that enjoys a coastline.

But the yacht has been more than a vessel of pleasure and sport. Over the years it has played a useful part in ship development. For instance the 10 gun brig was much improved for the Navy by yachtsmen in the 1830's. Then there is the dramatic event of the unofficial display of the new steam turbine in the TURBINIA at the Diamond Jubilee Review in 1897 which resulted in the new Royal Yacht ALEXANDRA subsequently being fitted with this revolutionary method of harnessing steam power.

This fascinating account of the development of yachting by Maldwin Drummond, himself a yachtsman of no mean renown, not only describes in detail the grand vessels but clearly illustrates that to the owner even the smallest yacht can be a 'salt-water palace'.

I shall certainly never forget the enormous pleasure I had in my 66 ton yacht SHRIMP both in northern and Mediterranean waters. I have since had five small motor yachts, my present one in Ireland being SHADOW V, all of which have given me equal pleasure.

This Introduction was completed by Lord Mountbatten a few days before his tragic death. We received this very sad news, with deep regret, as the book was going to press.

Bibliography

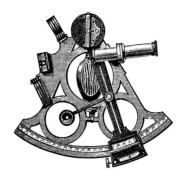

Atkins, J.B. (1939), *Further Memorials of the Royal Yacht Squadron (1901-1938)*, Geoffrey Bles
Bagot, A.G. (1888), *Shooting and Yachting in the Mediterranean*, W.H. Allen
Beaufort, Duke of, Editor (1894), *Yachting*, Longmans, Green & Co. (2 vols.)
Brassey, Anna (1886), *A Voyage in the 'Sunbeam'*, Longmans, Green & Co.
Childers, Erskine (1903), *The Riddle of the Sands*, Smith Elder & Co.
Condy, Mrs. N.M. (1884), *Reminiscences of a Yachting Cruise*, Hunt & Co.
Crabtree, R. (1973), *The Luxury Yacht*, David & Charles
Crabtree, R. (1975), *Royal Yachts of Europe*, David & Charles
Dodgson, Bowman W. (19—), *Yachting & Yachtsmen*, Geoffrey Bles
Dutton, T.G. (18—), *Yachting*, John B. Day
Gabe, Julius (1902), *Yachting*, John MacQueen
'The Governor' (1879), *A Yachtsman's Holidays*, Pickering & Co.
Grout, Jack (1978), *C'Etait en Temps des Yachtsmen*, Editions Gallimard
Guest, Montague (1903), *Memorials of the Royal Yacht Squadron*, John Murray
Heaton, Peter (1972), *A History of Yachting in Pictures*, Tom Stacey
Heckstall-Smith, R. (1929), *The Britannia and Her Contemporaries*, Methuen & Co.
Heckstall-Smith, R. (1955), *Sacred Cowes*, Anthony Blond
Herapath, Spencer (1975), *The Royal Yacht Squadron*, The Field
Herreshoff, L. Francis (1978), *An L. Francis Herreshoff Reader*, International Marine Publishing
Hoffman, Erik (1970), *The Steam Yachts*, Nautical Publishing Co.
Hunts Yachting Magazine, 1852-1886, Hunt & Co.
Illingworth, John H. (1968), *Twenty Challengers for the America's Cup*, Hollis & Carter
Inglefield, Commander E. (1853), *A Summer Search for Sir John Franklin*, Thomas Harrison
Irvine, John (1937), *The King's Britannia*, Seeley Service
Julyan, Herbert E. (1950), *Sixty Years of Yachts*, Hutchinson & Co.
Kemp, Dixon (1885), *Yacht Architecture*, Horace Cox
Kemp, Dixon (1891), *A Manual of Yacht & Boat Sailing* (2 vols.) Horace Cox
Lloyds Register of Yachts, 1886-1979, Lloyds Register of Shipping (82 vols.)
McClintock, Captain F.L. (1859), *Fate of Sir John Franklin*, John Murray
McGowan, Dr. A.P. (1953), *Royal Yachts,* National Maritime Museum
Moens, W.J.C. (1876), *Through France & Belgium*, Hurst & Blackett
Nichol, M.J. (1909), *Three Voyages of a Naturalist*, Witherby
Nicholson, John (1970), *Great Years in Yachting*, Nautical Publishing Co.
Owen, Roderic (1978), *The Fate of Franklin*, Hutchinson
Phillips-Birt, Douglas (1974), *The History of Yachting*, Elm Tree Books
Phillips-Birt, Douglas (1978), *The Cumberland Fleet*, Royal Thames Yacht Club
Robinson, Bill (1971), *Legendary Yachts*, David McKay Co. Inc.
Scott-Hughes, John (1928), *Famous Yachts*, Methuen
Shelley Rolls, Sir John (1932), *Lists of Members of the Royal Yacht Squadron and Their Yachts*, Zaehnsdorf, Ltd
Stephens, William P. (1942), *Traditions & Memories of American Yachting,* Motor Boating
Sutherland, Douglas (1965), *The Yellow Earl*, Cassell
'Vanderdecken' (18—), *The Yacht Sailor*, Hunt & Co.
H.M. Queen Victoria (1868), *Leaves from the Journal of Our Life in the Highlands from 1848-1861,* Smith Elder & Co
Young, A. (1879), *The Two Voyages of the Pandora*, Edward Stanford

Contents

Preface and Acknowledgements

An observant traveller in Europe may see the threads of history woven through town and countryside. The legacy of buildings from the Victorian and Edwardian periods is particularly rich. Their character may be inspected from within and without and, in some cases, little change has occurred. Wrought and cast iron decoration and street furniture act as islands of interest, remaining like rocks in the sand when the tide has gone out, as they sit among modern buildings. Even relics of transport are preserved in museums to allow the inquisitive to touch what great-grandmother put her fingers upon.

The sea is harsher and the mariner less careful of his vessel after it has served its purpose, whether for trade or pleasure. It is now very difficult to find a yacht that sailed the same waters and at the same time as the Royal Yacht VICTORIA & ALBERT II, broken up and burnt in 1904.

Twenty years ago a visit to a little port or small yachting centre would produce a feast for the eye, with little wooden vessels expressing the different ideas and needs of both designer and owner. Many were bright and cared for, others, nestling in the mud, were in various stages of neglect. A noticeable percentage of the smart yachts and hulks had experienced the water when Victoria was on the throne.

Now, every sheltered niche in our coastline is filled with serried ranks of plastic boats, owing much of their shape to the needs of the manufacturer and his production line, rather than to the whim of those who banded together, as in the old days, to create a yacht. A view through the masts used to be a particular delight, for there was expression there of infinite variety. The strength of modern materials has made a similar glimpse today an antiseptic experience. Even the flap of the halyards has lost that solid, reassuring note and is now octaves higher and irritating enough to bring threat of punishment under marina by-laws. The pleasure of going to sea is still there, but it is no longer so exciting for the spectator wandering the shore.

The real loss, though, is the view below. The warmth of timber has been replaced with cold materials more at home in a kitchen. The feel and atmosphere have disappeared and along with them the smell that could tell you instantly whether the boat was reasonably sound or suspiciously ripe. Much of the individuality has gone, too, for most production line manufacturers become 'marlin spike eyed' if anything not standard is requested by a purchaser with ideas of his own.

The title of this book, 'Salt-Water Palaces', would encourage the reader to feel that this concern with small boats is out of place, yet size is an incomplete guide when it comes to defining a 'salt-water palace', for such a description may reflect a personal feeling. A number of small yacht owners may think that such a label fits their little ship exactly. Chapter IV gives this idea historical backing.

This book is mostly devoted to the telling of magnificent vessels and the world that surrounded them. They were the ones that caused such a stir more than 65 years ago and now have virtually disappeared. The very few that have survived have been so very much altered that their original appearance inside and out is just a memory. Such ships were the

The Marquess of Ailsa
Miss Armett
'Brookie' Brooks-Baker
Kenneth Beken
Cdr. Errol Bruce
The Marquess of Bute
The Viscount Camrose
The Earl Cathcart, and the Committee
  of the Royal Yacht Squadron
David Couling
Elisabeth Darley-Doran
Ian Dear
Major Desmond Dillon
Bend'or Drummond
The Earl of Dunraven
Agustin Edwards
Malu Edwards
Graham Harvey-Evers
Molly Harvey-Evers
The Knight of Glin
Basil Greenhill
Rosalie Hendey
Spencer Herepath
Erik Hoffman
Roger Huggett
Robert Jarman
Lloyds Register of Shipping
David Lyon
Major Nigel Chamberlayne-Macdonald
Penelope Chamberlayne-Macdonald
Dr Alan McGowan
David Mathews
Diana Mathews
David May
John Millar
David Miller
Sir Iain Moncreiffe of That Ilk
Lord Montagu of Beaulieu
Mrs Moore
Captain John Mott, R.N.,
Colin Mudie
Rosemary Mudie
The Trustees of the National Maritime Museum
The National Trust for Scotland
Bertram Newbury
Christopher Nicholson
The Librarian of the Oceanographic
  Museum, Monaco
George Pattinson
Air Commodore 'Paddy' Quinnell
The Radio Times Hulton Picture Library
Royal Thames Yacht Club
The Librarian of the Scott Polar
  Research Institute
Sir Geoffrey Shackerley
Colonel Robert Steele
The late Duke of Westminster
John White

very best that the Victorian and Edwardian shipbuilder could produce and were the equivalent of the great houses on land. Such marvellous expression in wood and iron was mirrored by the behaviour of their owners. The purpose of this book is to guide the reader gently below, down the carved companion way, wandering on rich carpet from saloon to stateroom, listening to conversations about yachts and more yachts, their owners and how they gathered together into clubs. The story starts with Charles II and gathers momentum through the great years of Victoria and Edward VII, stretching to the beginning of the First War, when that period really ended. The conversations die then, not because large yachts and interesting people did not continue to exist after that date, for they did. This book leaves out, for example, the 407' overall SAVARONA III, 4,317 tons T.M., built for Mrs Emily Cadwalader at a cost of $4,000,000, for she was launched in 1930. The barque HUSSAR, later SEA CLOUD, PATRIA and ANTARNA, 2,990 tons T.M., is not covered for she was built for Mrs Marjorie Hutton by Frederick Krupp in 1931. The great Herreschoff designed schooner WESTWARD, 323 tons T.M. that carried 13,455 square feet of sail was built in 1910, but her great period was between the wars. Her day really started when she was bought in 1924 by that fine and robust sailor T.B.F. Davis and raced against the Royal cutter BRITANNIA. But in spite of all this, the world had changed gear after the First Great War and the closing down sale had begun by 1920.

Many still have records and mementoes from the days before 1914 scattered about. Sometimes treasured, sometimes unhung, are the works of the great yachting photographers – W.U. Kirk and Sons, Beken and Debenham, all of Cowes. Less well known were G. West & Sons of Southsea and Gosport, J. Adamson & Son of Rothesay and W. Roberts & Co. of Gourock and Glasgow. Of the great photographers, only Beken survives. This firm possesses, with the great American company started by Morris Rosenfeld, the world's finest collections of yacht photographs. Any researcher into the history of yachts or, indeed, touching on yachts at all, must have reason to be in their debt.

Private albums, filled with picture memories, have also been a valuable resource for this book and their owners, who have been of great assistance are listed, with grateful thanks. In addition, there are many others to whom adequate appreciation is difficult to give, for they have lent their knowledge, time and archives, and opened their houses, so combining to make this book possible. Their names are also to be found in the list.

I would also like to thank those authors and publishers who have been kind enough to let me quote from their works. I have included a comprehensive bibliography and made reference to each author and his book in the text. The bibliography also forms a recommended list for further reading.

I have reserved the last word to express my particular gratitude to Lord Mountbatten for contributing the Introduction. He is our finest sailor and must be numbered among the most celebrated of these islands. The amateur always looks to the professional for inspiration and guidance and the yachtsman is no exception.

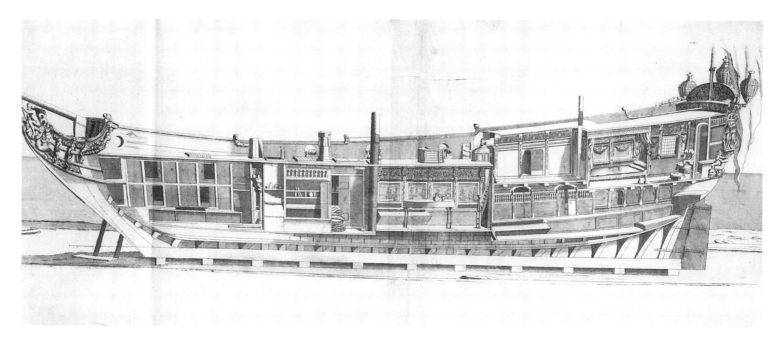

A cutaway drawing by Coronelli showing the accommodation of an unnamed royal yacht of 1693. (National Maritime Museum)

The Royal Yacht MARY was England's first true yacht. Thirty men and eight guns were crammed aboard her 52 foot gilded hull. MARY was wrecked on March 25th, 1675 and rediscovered by members of the British Sub-Aqua Club on July 11th, 1971. (National Maritime Museum)

CHAPTER 1

Royal Patronage

Caligula was fond of sailing. He is credited by Suetonius with owning a yacht, to use a term that was to come in sixteen hundred or so years later. Whether his sailing expenses were the reason that he dipped so deeply into Tiberius' treasury his biographer does not say, but such records show that sailing for pleasure was a royal sport about the time of Christ. Boating, to use a less noble term, has been man's recreation since he lay on his first log, and so may claim to be one of the oldest water pastimes, if not sports.

To the Vikings, ships were weapons. They were no doubt used relatively peacefully on state occasions. The early development of pleasure vessels owes half parentage to royal pleasure and half to state requirements. This last use was, and perhaps still is, the national effort to entertain the unentertainable.

Those responsible for state or, indeed, Navy ships' names certainly had a flare. How else could they have called the little vessel built at Cowes for 'national entertainment' purposes in the year of the Armada, 1588, RAT o'WIGHT. This was nearly three-quarters of a century before Evelyn records in his diary for October 1st, 1661:

> 'I sailed this morning with His Majesty in one of his yachts, vessels not known among us till the Dutch East India Company presented that curious piece to the King; being very excellent sailing vessels. It was on a wager between his other new pleasure boat, built frigate-like, and one of the Duke of York's, the wager £100, the race from Greenwich to Gravesend and back. The King lost it going, the wind being contrary, but saved stakes in returning. There were divers noble persons and lords on board, His Majesty sometimes steering himself.'

This short paragraph marks the foundation of British yachting, the new word coming with the vessel, for *jaght* was a 17th century Dutch term formed on *jagen*, to hunt or chase. A *jachtschip* was a 'ship for chasing'. This soon became 'yacht' and the word attained great popularity, growing with the royal sport. It is interesting to look a little further, for a person enjoying being on the water for pleasure was then a 'yachtman'. 'Yachtsman' is a 19th century bending of the word.

Charles II did not suddenly become a yachtman and discover the sea as part of his pursuit of pleasure. He had sheltered in the Scillies and Channel Islands, spending some time sailing amongst them for amusement while avoiding the Roundheads. When his fortunes failed again at the Battle of Worcester on September 3rd, 1651, he went on a roundabout land route to Brighton, arriving there on October 15th when he boarded the coasting brig SURPRISE. Captain Tattersall took him to Fécamp.

A decade later, after the Restoration, he bought the brig and renamed her ROYAL ESCAPE. The King, remembering her service to him, had her anchored off the Palace of Whitehall, where she was open to royal visitors. ROYAL ESCAPE, ex SURPRISE, could, therefore, take pride in being the first museum ship, though she catered for a rare public.

MARY did not come to him by chance either. Charles expressed considerable interest in the small vessel and this led to the presentation of MARY. Charles' absorption with yachting was fuelled by his rousing send-off and homecoming in the little Dutch Admiralty yacht and his adventures as a fugitive. These combined to put salt in his blood.

Pepys records how he visited MARY in November of 1660 and writes that she 'is one of the finest things I ever saw for neatness and room in so small a vessel'.

John Evelyn and Samuel Pepys give glimpses of these early days in the annals of yachting. Evelyn was born in 1620, some 13 years before Pepys, who became a great friend. They worked together when Pepys was Secretary to the Admiralty and Evelyn was serving on a commission of inquiry into sick and wounded mariners of Charles' Dutch Wars (1665-1667 and 1672-1674). Evelyn kept his diary for over 50 years, starting when he was 11, while Pepys' celebrated and more lively record was for only 10 years between 1660 and 1669.

MARY was 52′ on the keel, with a draught of only 3′. She carried lee boards in the Dutch manner. Thirty men and eight guns were crammed aboard England's first true yacht. The royal quarters were aft, in a great cabin under the poop deck. Elaborate carving, highly gilded, decorated everything, as can be seen from the illustration. Her crowning glory was the figurehead, a unicorn. MARY was named after the Princess Royal, mother of William III. She was wrecked on a foggy night on March 25th, 1675 when she struck a rock near the present Skerries lighthouse, seven miles from Holyhead. She carried a crew of 28 and 46 passengers, including the Earl of Ardglass, the Earl of Meath and his son Lord Ardee. Her wreck was rediscovered on July 11th, 1971 by divers from the Chorley and Merseyside branches of the British Sub-Aqua Club and a considerable number of artifacts were recovered. (P.N. Davies, 1973 Int. Journal of Nautical Archaeology & Underwater Exploration 2.1:59.73)

There were three other yachts in the royal fleet, competing and cruising the Thames in this first yachting year. KATHERINE, again owned by the King, was of English construction to designs of Commissioner Phineas Pett and named after the King's wife to be, Katherine of Braganza. ANNE belonged to Charles' brother, the Duke of York, Lord High Admiral. She appears to be a near sister to MARY, though designed by Phineas' brother, Christopher, and took her name from the Duke's wife. The last yacht was BEZAN, a small Dutch-built vessel of only 34′ on the keel, yet carrying four guns. BEZAN was a trial horse, as it were, and the most successful of the four, in spite of being much the smallest. Her mainsail was set on a small gaff with a long boom, an aspect which is still to be seen in Holland today. Commander C. Gavin in 'Royal Yachts' hails BEZAN as the origin of the bermudan rig. Her name comes from the Dutch word for small yacht.

To these four little ships and to Charles II we owe the popularity of yachting, but credit for the modern idea of sailing for pleasure must go to the Dutch.

Charles' triumphant passage from Breda to Delft, stopping briefly at Rotterdam, was accomplished by water. For at least part of the journey the retinue consisted of 13 yachts. The following account comes from Adrian Vlackett, writing in 1660.

> 'Each yacht had her own steward, cooks, and officers who were in charge of the pantry, kitchen and 'wines, and those yachts which had not suitable kitchens on board were accompanied by other vessels, wherein stoves for the kitchen had been provided, also ovens for baking, and there had been made great provision of so great a quantity of all kinds of food, game, confitures, and wines, and all the tables were so fully served, that the stewards of the English lords, though accustomed to abundance, were astonished thereat, and confessed that they could not conceive by what means twenty or twenty-five great dishes for each table could be prepared on board the yachts and with the motion of the water.'

It is certainly clear from this account that yachting was for pleasure, and not just that attained by silent progress with sun on the back and wind on the cheek.

The concept of a kitchen boat was Dutch and Charles obtained the idea from them. The ketch ROE was pressed into culinary service and renamed ROE KITCHEN before Charles built one of his own in 1670. This was perhaps the strangest of all royal yachts. Though highly decorated, and carrying six guns in peace and eight in war, she received no favours when it came to her name – KITCHEN.

Early yachtsmen, royal or otherwise, were as keen on comfort as they were on food. They also employed ways of passing time when deserted by the wind, as Pepys records in his diary for August 17th, 1665:

> 'After dinner we went down by boat to Greenwich to the BEZAN yacht where Sir W. Batten, Sir J. Minnes, My Lord Bruncker (President of the Royal Society) and myself, with some servants, embarked in the yacht, and down we went most pleasantly. Short of Graves End it grew calme, and we come to an anchor and to supper mighty merry and after it, being moonshine, we out of the cabin to laugh and talk, and then, as we grew sleepy, went in, and upon velvet cushions of the King's that belonged to the yacht, fell to sleep, which we all did pretty well till three or four of the clock, having risen in the night to look for a new comet which is said to have lately shone, but we could see no such thing.'

Shore diversions, such as cards, were a favourite too and the sounds of a sleeping ship have not changed much either, judging by Pepys' memory of October 1st, 1665:

> 'We breakfasted betimes and come to the fleet about 2 o'clock in the afternoon, having a fine day and fine wind. My Lord received us mighty kindly... After supper on board the BEZAN, and there to cards for a while, and then to read and so to sleep. But Lord! The mirth which it caused me to be waked in the night by their snoring round me; I did laugh till I was ready to burst, and waked one, who could not a good while tell where he was when he heard one laugh so, till he recollected himself, and I told him what it was at, and so to sleep again, they still snoring.'

However, these cruises on the Thames were not always so joyful, judging from Lady Batten's reaction or Pepys' own memories of seasickness. Pepys records for September 3rd, 1663 how he, accompanied by Sir William and Lady Batten, sailed from Greenwich eastward to the Downs, the anchorage inside the Goodwin Sands between North and South Foreland. Lady Batten was not much of a sailor and the trip ended with her being put ashore at Queenborough, Isle of Sheppey vowing that she would never go to sea again. Pepys suspected that things would not go well, as he writes:

> 'The winde very fresh, and I believe they will be all sicke enough, besides that she is mighty troublesome on the water.'

He was, of course, referring to Lady Batten rather than the yacht CHARLOTTE.

His own stomach was tender, too, on occasions, as he confesses when visiting the PRINCE, flagship of Lord Sandwich, on September 18th, 1665.

> 'Sir W. Penn stayed to dine and did so, but the wind being high the ship (though the motion of it was hardly discernible to the eye) did make me sick, so that I could not eat anything almost...and so to our yacht again. No sooner come into the yacht, though overjoyed with the good work we have done today, but I was overcome with seasickness so that I began to spue soundly and so continued a good while, till at last I went into the cabin, and shutting my eyes my trouble did cease that I fell asleep, which continued till we come into Chatham River where the water was smooth, and then I rose and was very well.'

He was not always as seasick as this, as he records in an earlier reminiscence which certainly shows how keen the Restoration yachtsmen were on their stomachs, whatever their sufferings.

> 'We went down four or five miles (below Woolwich) with extraordinary pleasure, it being a fine day and a brave gale of wind, and had some oysters brought us aboard newly taken, which were **excellent**, and ate with great pleasure. There also coming into the river two

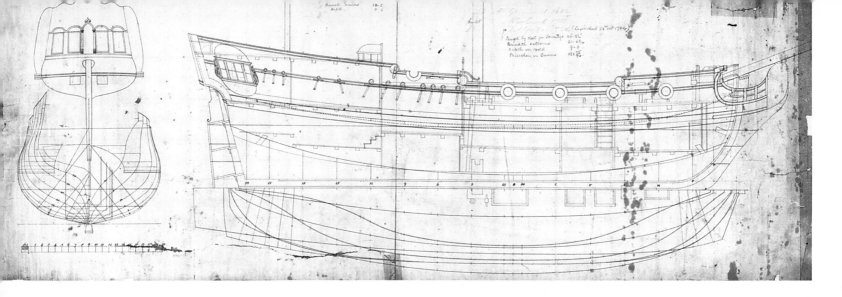

Dutchmen, we sent a couple of men on board and bought three Holland's cheeses, cost 4d apiece, excellent cheeses.'

The high living on board was complemented by the standard of decoration, both within and without. Everything was done to ensure that the royal yacht looked the part and as they were ships of state, this was clearly important. The yacht's presence at sea and in harbour should not go unnoticed. This has been a matter of prime importance in all royal yachts of any nationality or age. Falconer in his Marine Dictionary of 1780 makes the point as part of his definition: 'They are in general elegantly furnished, and richly ornamented with sculpture; and always commanded by captains in His Majesty's Navy.'

Such rich carving and gilded ornament stretched from the figurehead to the stern galleries. British Royal yachts, followed such tradition until this century. The figurehead was inherited directly from the custom of ancient Egypt, where such ornament, usually the head or figure of a bird, gave a soul to the vessel and complemented the idea that ships were living things. The animal's eyes were regarded as a navigational aid, for with them the ship could see where she was going. The highly ornamented beakhead, however, was usually devoted to a less elegant purpose – the seaman's lavatory. The word 'heads comes from beakhead and ladders or hatches led straight from the fo'c'sle. The sea saw to it that this highly ornamented and sanitary position was kept well washed.

Further aft the circular gun ports were wreathed in carved and gilded wood and the quarter and stern galleries were treated in the same exotic way.

A glance at the drawing of FUBBS shows the attention to detail and the care and love that went into the building of the most ornamental vessel yet devised. It is worth looking at FUBBS for she was Charles II's finest and favourite yacht. She was not only good to look at but weatherly as well.

FUBBS was built at Greenwich in 1682 by Sir Phineas Pett and rigged as a ketch, an arrangement said to have been invented by Charles II especially for yachts. She was by no means the largest of Charles' pleasure vessels. That honour, usually accorded to the new MARY, actually belonged to SANDADOES (meaning 'intense longing' in Portuguese) of 180 tons burden and 74' along the keel. FUBBS was a little smaller, 148 tons and 73' 6'' on the keel. For armament she carried 12 three pounder guns and boasted of a crew of 30.

Charles called her after Louise de Kerouaille, Duchess of Portsmouth, who was a particular favourite of his. FUBBS was her pet name, coming from the Old English 'Fubby' which has the meaning of 'Chubby' today. Charles used FUBBS a good deal and one of his last cruises was taken in her in 1680, down river and around the North Foreland. The account of this voyage was published in 1776 in 'A History of Music' by Dr Charles Burney.

He recalls how the King had invited the Rev. John Gostling, one of his Deans at the Chapel Royal and a Canon of Canterbury, aboard. As they made their way eastward, John Gostling sang with the King. Charles much admired Gostling's voice, for on one occasion he rewarded him with a silver egg filled with golden guineas, remarking at the time that eggs were good for the voice.

As FUBBS rounded the North Foreland, the weather changed and a strong breeze sprang up, soon reaching gale force. The King and the Duke of York had to leave the poop and lend a hand, joining the crew to save their vessel. They struggled into Ramsgate. Gostling was so relieved that as a sort of votive offering, giving thanks for delivery to God, he wrote the words of the anthem 'They That Go Down to the Sea in Ships'. He persuaded his friend Henry Purcell to set them to music.

FUBBS continued in the royal service long after Charles' death. She accompanied William III to Holland and was used as a despatch vessel by the Navy. In 1696 she was in action and played her part in the 'burning of the town on Cadinall Island'.

FUBBS was rebuilt three times – in 1701, 1729 and again in 1749. She was finally broken up in 1781. Parts of her had served King and country for 99 years – no mean record.

The Royal yacht demanded respect from lesser vessels. Other ships were required to dip their ensigns, or strike colours when passing the King's vessel. On one occasion, while the HENRIETTA (built in 1663, 52' on the keel, 104 tons burden) was fitting out, a passing merchantman failed to give such a signal of respect. The crew of the royal yacht seized the offending vessel and demanded payment of a fine. However, the authorities thought the royal sailors had overstepped the mark, as the King was not aboard and so ordered her release.

The cost of yachts and yachting certainly commanded respect too. Charles built, bought or altered nearly 30 yachts in his lifetime. However, as these little ships were also required for naval and other state duties they did not cause a drain on the privy purse.

Charles' yachts were expensive to build. The original estimate for the HENRIETTA, for example, was £1,850 without guns, according to the calendar of state papers – Domestic, 1663. She was fitted out economically, too, for below instead of carved panelling, which was traditional, it is recorded that the bulkheads and deckheads were of gilded leather.

The building costs of two of Charles' vessels – the ANNE and the CHARLES – were researched and recorded by the Yachtsman's Publishing Company in their magnificent book 'British Yachts and Yachtsmen' published in 1909.

				Anne			*Little Charles*		
				£	s	d	£	s	d
Hull	...	...	...	1,815	2	4	722	1	5
Rig	...	...	...	240	12	0	147	2	0
Lead	...	...	...	324	0	0	159	13	7
Guns	...	...	...	186	9	10	120	0	0
Colours	...	...	...				128	13	6
				2,566	4	2	1,277	10	6

ANNE was 100 tons burden and 52′ on the keel while CHARLES was 38 tons and 36′ on the keel. This means that CHARLES cost £33.13s a ton while ANNE worked out at £25.13s a ton. However, the cost may well have been more in the case of ANNE. The method of calculating tonnage at that time was length of Keel × Beam × Depth, over 94 = Tonnage. Using this formula, ANNE appears to have been 73.5 tons and would have, therefore, cost nearly £40 a ton to build, which is a very high figure for that time. A man of war at the time of the Restoration, ready for sea, would have cost £15 a ton, while a merchant vessel came in at about £8 a ton.

It is interesting to note that a set of flags cost more than the guns. They probably consisted of a standard, Admiralty flag, ensign and numerous pennants. The flags would have been made of silk, which accounts for the surprising size of the bill. Large flags were much in vogue, for they were important for proper recognition from afar. It may have taken an age to tack after or chase a ship. Flags of today's proportions would have made such action necessary, so large ensigns or signals were practical as aids to identification, particularly for messages within the fleet. The rule was, the more important the ship, the larger the flag, and the King's yacht would have been overwhelmed in silk to ensure proper recognition. This may account for the rage of the crew of the HENRIETTA, for such lack of response was poor return after their Royal master had invested so much in luxurious signal.

As to running costs, the principal call was wages and they were low at that time. An able seaman in the Navy would draw 24 shillings a month. The bill for ANNE's complement of 12 men for 22 months 6 days on April 19th, 1661 came to £801. This averages out at £3.00 a month or two shillings a day per man. Compared with the Navy, the crew of Royal yachts were significantly better off.

If Royal yachting was expensive, prize money for races was good, but such return appeared to be more by way of wager than regular prize. As seen at the beginning of the chapter, a wager of £100 was mentioned for the race between Greenwich and Gravesend. On another occasion, the competition between KATHERINE and ANNE, ANNE won the leg to Gravesend earning £50, but the advantage was again wiped out by KATHERINE on the way home.

It would be wrong, though, to label yacht racing in those early days as purely a royal pastime or the cruises as regal recreation, spiced sometimes with diplomatic or naval purpose. The yacht race was often the best method of gauging the success or otherwise of a new idea. The King's yacht could also be despatched for particular purpose without upsetting the regime or strength of the fleet. Charles II, as the principal advocate of the sport and being keen on naval development as well, was often intimately involved. Two remarkable men helped him in this and the King's yachts enabled them to further their ideas.

The first of these was Sir William Petty (1623-1687). He was one of the most gifted men of his time.

William Petty went to sea at an early age but his talents were too great for one element. He returned to the beach and achieved the remarkable scholastic record of being both professor of anatomy at Oxford and music in London. As if this was not enough, he was an Irish M.P. and landowner. However, Petty's great talent and claim to fame was as a political economist and an inventor. He was perhaps the first European to develop the catamaran (TAMIL – *catta* = tie; *maram* = wood) and was certainly the first to race a twin-hulled vessel in British waters. A match was organised to prove the superior speed of such a design which took place in Dublin Bay, under the auspices of the Royal Society, on January 12th, 1663. Petty's trial horse competed against a barge belonging to the King, a man'o'war's boat and 'a large black pleasure boat' according to Birches' 'History of the Royal Society'. Petty described the twin hulls of his vessel as 'cylinders' and this may well have been an accurate description.

The 'cylinder catamaran' had the legs on the others down wind to such a degree that her poor performance later to windward hardly mattered. She broke one of her rudders clawing off a lee shore but the large black pleasure boat, her nearest rival, lost her boom and Petty's invention carried the day, claiming the Royal Society's prize flag.

Sir William developed his ideas further in the years that followed as reported in the paper 'Mercurius Publicus' for August 6th, 1663.

> 'You must pardon me if I hit not the Sea phrases, but in plain English the matter is thus. On Wednesday this new Device which the people severally call the INVENTION, others the MERCURY, others the GEMINI, others the CASTOR & POLLUX, others the ZABULON NAPHTHALY, others the WIT & MONEY, etc. returned the second time from Holyhead on Wednesday, 22nd instant about 5 in the afternoone, directly against the wind. She had set out from thence with the OSSORY Ketch, the most famed of all our three Pacquet Boats, and to which we are most beholding for the speedy transport of our Letters, especially in contrary Winds, but arrived 16 hours before the said Ketch, whom she ran out of sight and left to Leeward. In a watch of 4 houres time, whereby we guesse that she outdoes ordinary vessels halfe in halfe.'

The paper goes on to wonder about the problems of keeping the hulls together in much the same vain as the modern critic of the multi-hull. The paper continues with these words:

> 'Upon these experiments most gainsayers are now silent, objecting only the excessive charge of building her and of men to Sayle her, and the danger of separation of her bodies in a Storme but as to charge, let the author looke to it and the passengers to the danger of separation.'

With the further development of this then novel craft, Sir William's 'cylinders' were given the more dignified name of a 'sluice-boat'. His EXPERIMENT sank in severe weather in the Irish Channel on her return from London, where she had been inspected by the King. Petty's last 'sluice', ST. MICHAEL, was a signal failure. C.H. Hull in his book on Petty damns her magnificently. His words echo the feelings of yacht owners down the ages when looking back on their new yacht's first calendar of disappointments.

> 'His (Petty's) new vessel, however, performed as abmominably as if built on purpose to disappoint in the highest degree every particular that was expected of her.'

Pepys did not think much of catamarans either.

The other Restoration sailor to use a royal yacht to push forward the frontiers of knowledge was Captain Greenvile Collins who died in 1693, the year that his 'Great Britain's Coasting Pilot' was first published. This remarkable volume was the first ever survey of the sea coast of Britain. He paid tribute to his royal master in the preface to the reader:

> 'His Most Excellent Majesty, King Charles II, who was a great lover of the nobel art of navigation, finding that there were no Sea-Charts or Maps of these kingdoms but what were Dutch, and Copies from them, and those very erroneous, His Majesty out of his great Zeal for the better improvement of navigation, was pleased in the year 1682, to give me the command of a Yacht for the making this survey; in which Service I spent Seven Years time.'

Collins used two royal yachts for the purpose. He employed MERLIN of 53′ on the

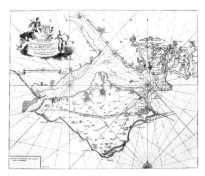

The Isle of Wight and the Solent by Captain Greenvile Collins from his 'Great Britain's Coasting Pilot' 1693. (Cadland Archives)

keel from 1681 to 1683 and MONMOUTH of 52' on the keel from 1683 to 1688. Both were built on the Thames in 1666, the year of the Great Fire of London. With them he produced 120 harbour and shore plans, 48 of which were included in the Pilot. Collins was certainly the right man for the job, for he had been 'Master' or navigating officer aboard SWEEPSTAKES under Sir John Narborough on his voyage round the Horn to the west coast of South America from 1669 to 1671, just 100 years after Drake's epic achievement.

The Pilot ran to twelve editions and was used throughout the 18th century. Collins and his surveys in Charles' royal yachts enabled British and foreign masters, unfamiliar with a particular harbour or coastline around Britain, to navigate safely.

Charles II recommended the sea to his people for pleasure. He saw that there were three principal sides to the pastime – racing, cruising and the use of the yacht to advance knowledge of the sea and ships. He understood comfort at the same time and, with the help of the Dutch, created the Salt-Water Palace.

With the death of Charles II in 1685 the wind of pleasure faltered and died away. Yachting was in the doldrums and remained becalmed for nearly a hundred years. Royal patronage seemed essential to keep the sport moving. Yachts were built for the Crown and used extensively but were affairs of state; pleasure was coincidental. However, the Royal ships were not a backwater and the Crown employed their very best officers to command their yachts on these state occasions.

Lord Anson (1697-1762) was perhaps the most illustrious. He was not only an Admiral of the Fleet but First Lord of the Admiralty when he had charge of the royal yachts. He conveyed both George II and George III across the Channel and in 1749 brought the latter's Queen, Princess Charlotte Mecklenburg-Strelitz, to these shores.

The Princess must have been a good sailor, for the passage back from Stade aboard the ROYAL CHARLOTTE, ex ROYAL CAROLINE and renamed in her honour, was not without incident. The royal yacht was nearly driven north to Norway by successive southwesterly gales and yet it is recorded:

> 'Notwithstanding the fatigue of the voyage, the Princess amused herself with playing the harpsichord and continued in good spirits and health, endearing herself to all on board by her fascinating manners.'

ROYAL CHARLOTTE was only 72' 2" on the keel.

The ROYAL CHARLOTTE aboard which George III's Queen 'amused herself with playing the harpsichord' on her way from Stade to England, in spite of gales driving her nearly to Norway. (National Maritime Museum)

Whether it was the Queen's enthusiasm for the sea or her tolerance of its ways that led to George III's enthusiasm for the water is not known. George was certainly keen on naval reviews and promoted them as a way of improving the Navy in both substance and morale. His brother, Henry Frederick, Duke of Cumberland enjoyed sailing and started the Cumberland Fleet in 1775, as we shall learn later.

The eleven years between 1794 and 1805 were the most celebrated in Britain's naval history. The Glorious First of June in 1794 took place in the North Atlantic and saw the defeat of Admiral Louis Villaret de Joyeuse and at the end of little more than a decade, on October 21st, 1805, came the most famous naval victory of all time – Nelson's destruction of the Franco-Spanish fleet off Cape Trafalgar.

It would have been difficult during those stirring times not to have been carried away by what was happening at sea. Perhaps because of this many made their way to the coast and the era of the seaside holiday began. At that time, however, people preferred to be in the sea rather than on it. George III, though, was an exception and was particularly fond of yachting at Weymouth. The royal yachts ROYAL CHARLOTTE and PRINCESS AUGUSTA were those most favoured by the King. In the summer of 1801 he required the royal yacht

AUGUSTA, with the necessary escorts of the frigates HYDRA, under Captain the Hon. Charles Paget, and FORTUNE, commanded by Lord Amelius Beauclerc, to await his pleasure off Weymouth. A biography of William Mark, purser, Royal Navy, in the book 'At Sea with Nelson' published in 1929 gives an insight into royal celebrations afloat in that year.

'I perceive that the officers considered this an expensive and unprofitable service: full dress every day, and no prize money to be made. The King went frequently to sea in his yacht. The two frigates kept close company, and always passed the yacht on the opposite tacks. To make the cruise pleasant the vessels were always beating, whichever way the wind was. The bands of music were always playing, and the thing was in many respects very agreeable.

'This affair lasted more than three months and previous to its breaking up Captain Paget resolved to give a ball and dinner to the Royal family, with the nobility and gentry then at Weymouth. The ship was for some days being prepared. The spanker boom was removed, and a table in the form of a horseshoe was placed about the mizzen mast especially for the Royal family. The guns on the main deck were stowed fore and aft, and tables were made on both sides for the nobility and gentry, while the quarter deck was kept purposely for the dancing.

'The day arrived. The Royal family and company came on board, making altogether a pretty stout party. The dancing commenced immediately and continued for two or three hours, during which the good old King walked about and asked questions, which, of course, there was always someone at hand to answer. On expressing a desire to see some of the ship's company's beer, a barrel was hoisted up, and being lowered on the fife-rail at the front of the quarter deck and tapped, he had a tumbler presented to him. I cannot exactly say what opinion he did express as to its quality, but it certainly was most ordinary hogwash.

'The ball subsided for a time and everyone went to dinner, the King being seated at the centre of the horseshoe table and the rest of the Royal family down the two sides. They were waited on by Captain Paget as the host; his father, the Earl of Uxbridge, as Page in Waiting, and other pages. They appeared to eat and drink very much like other people. The officers were stationed at different sections of the long tables on the main deck to preserve order and to see that no attention to the guests was omitted. We, the Petty Officers, had a most comfortable table laid for us in the gun room and there was no want of anything. Captain Paget had a very good Irish piper on board, who generally played to the Captain and Officers at their dinner time. He had a capital set of Union Pipes with keys, imitating all the sweet tones of the flute. By Mr Colquitt's (the First Lieutenant) idea a stage was comprised and slung over the taffrail, on which O'Farrel was placed of course entirely out of sight. In the middle of dinner he struck up "God Save the King". This drew everyone's attention, and no one knew where the sound came from. "Rule Britannia" followed and many more beautiful aires, O'Farrel acquitting himself well. Everyone seemed delighted from the King downwards.'

By 1803, ROYAL CHARLOTTE was a ripe age of 54 years. It was decided to replace her with a larger vessel, ROYAL SOVEREIGN. The Naval Chronicle of 1804 describes the launching ceremony:

'At a quarter before three o'clock on Saturday, May 12th, 1804, the new yacht built on purpose for His Majesty was launched from the King's Dock Yard at Deptford. She is a very neat but small ship. In her present trim she draws about 9' forward and 10' abaft. She is completely copper bottomed, as above that a streak of yellow and then another of blue, ornamented with medallions representing the four cardinal virtues, as female figures, in gilt frames. Over them there is a rich ornament of leaves entwined together, highly gilt. The figurehead is a representation of Her Majesty with the Imperial Crown over her head. This is

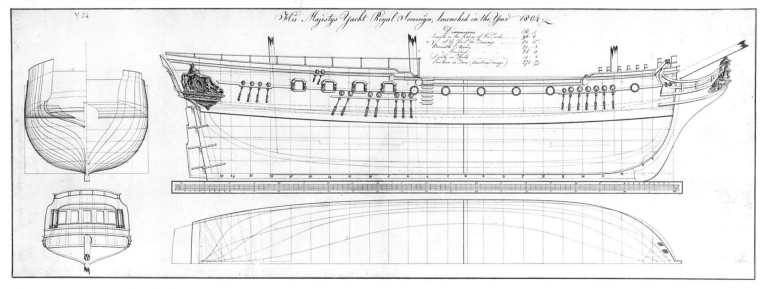

The ROYAL SOVERIEGN *was launched in 1804. The stern is decorated with Neptune in his car. The Master kicked a visitor from her quarter-deck for insulting His Majesty, King George III.* (National Maritime Museum)

encompassed by an iron railing to prevent any injury. The stern is decorated with the figure of Neptune in his Car, with his Trident in his hand and the Sea underneath and Dolphins playing around. Over the cabin windows and under the taffrail are placed the figures of the Four Quarters of the world over all. The accommodation ladder and the differing gratings are painted yellow, with very rich mouldings of carved work highly gilt. Upon the whole, as the sailors term it, there is an abundance of gingerbread work. The apartments laid out for the Royal family, as might be expected, are most sumptuous. The wood work is chiefly mahogany or cedar, with satin curtains, velvet seats, etc.'

One of the most amusing and descriptive accounts of life aboard a Royal yacht in the early part of the 19th century is supplied by Captain John H. Boteler in his privately printed biography, 'Recollections of My Sea Life'. He is recalling some 60 years later his appointment and first days aboard His Majesty's yacht ROYAL SOVEREIGN, then refitting at Deptford.

'When moored in the river we had several visitors, and one day a large wherry with silk awnings and cushions, and with six men in nautical dresses, and party of ladies, rowed slowly round us. I invited them to see the yacht and offered my arm to the best-looking lady and took her round the ship. All at once there was shout of "A man overboard!" The cries ran like wildfire; the ladies began to scream. I ran on deck, found the master, a fiery-eyed, red-faced little Welshman, in a great state of excitement. "What's all this, Franklin?" "I couldn't help it, sir; he began to abuse the King, and I hustled him to the gangway meaning to kick him into his boat, but she had dropped astern and overboard he went." And there he was, his bald head above water, paddling and splashing like a dog. A wherry took him up, and he would be landed. By this time some of the other men began to show their teeth. I told them to be silent, that any person who presumed to abuse His Majesty on board his own yacht would inevitably be kicked overboard by the officers, and so they all with great haste hustled into their boat. As it turned out they were not gentry. This never got into the papers; it would have gone well with Franklin had it reached the King's ears. Franklin told me that on showing the man the companion, a richly decorated staircase, as the entrance to the royal apartments, "Ah!" said the fellow, "just the thing for fat George when beastly drunk to roll down." "What, sir! How dare you sir! To abuse His Majesty on his own quarterdeck, and before one of his officers! Go along, sir, out of the ship, sir!" And so it ended. It was a lesson to us; we always afterwards required a card to be sent up before we admitted visitors, at least, questionable ones.

The yacht arrived in Antwerp and Boteler and others went sightseeing. They hired a *voiture* and a pair of horses and set out for Brussels, where they met up with their Captain

ROYAL SOVEREIGN was richly gilt, and the hull purple, the royal colour. Her gun parts were all circular, decorated with carved figures, the size of a two-year-old child. National Maritime Museum)

at the Hôtel de Flandre. Boteler's plan was to visit the Battlefield of Waterloo and his Captain thought it a splendid idea and joined the party. Seven years had gone by since the fight and the effects of the battle were everywhere – 'Branches torn off the trees, walls broken down, and at two farms La Belle Alliance and La Haye Sainte, the barn doors were riddled by bullets.' Boteler continues in a more macabre vein:

'The fields were well covered with luxuriant crops of young corn, and, on my noticing several patches of wheat of darker colour and a foot higher than the rest, La Coste said "Very reech, very reech, sir", and he made us understand that bodies of dead men and horses were there buried. In Waterloo church we were shown a small slab over the grave of the Marquess of Anglesey's leg.'

When the narrator arrived back on board, he found the crew had taken advantage of the Captain's and his absence:

'When I got on board I found the yacht's crew stupid as owls from the lot of Holland's drunk; very cheap here so I at once took strong measures against any further tippling, by having the Master At Arms at the gangway, knocking holes in stone jars and slitting bladders of spirit. I was informed that this was only meant for their wives at home. After a little I thought it a pity to waste so much good stuff, so had all future seizures put into "breakers" and when any extra work or bad weather happened, the "main brace was spliced", in plain English a tot was served all round; this quite won the hearts of our fine crew and won me high praise. When our Captain returned, we up anchor, worked down river, and in quick time were up the Thames again, expecting to be laid up, instead of which to our great delight, for yacht service was very fascinating, our Captain, Charlie Adam, joined, and we next day were off for Dover Roads, and in a day or so embarked the Crown Prince of Denmark and suite for Calais. On their leaving the yacht a diamond ring was presented to the Captain and 100 sovereigns to me for the ship's crew, and which I gave the purser to be distributed among them as prize money. I got into conversation with one of the party, a Danish nobleman Count Alterbourg, I think, and speaking of my three years service in the Great Belt, and of the island Romsoe, "Oh!" he exclaimed "That is my property. I had a cottage there, but there were so many English men of war about, and such frequent landing of seamen, that I was obliged to abandon it."

'In Calais Harbour we lashed alongside the pier. A French officer without a word to us, planted a sentry at the landing brow to prevent anyone coming on board unless passed by an officer. A gentleman, a Lieutenant Foley, whom I knew, wanted to come on board, and began to argue the point with the soldier, who, with scant ceremony, progged him in the stomach with the butt of his musket, doubling up poor Foley for the rest of the afternoon. Among our visitors were Beau Brummel and Tilney Long Wellesley Pole, or however those names may properly stand. We invited both to dine, Mr Pole declined, saying he was going home to an early dinner, seven o'clock, this to our unsophisticated minds seemed utter nonsense, and he also informed us that his creditors had allowed him sufficient to pay his shoe black; £2,000 a year! Mr Brummel accepted and was most entertaining.

'We returned to England and were ordered to Sheerness to be in readiness to join the ROYAL GEORGE yacht, about taking the King to Scotland.'

The Monarch was not, therefore, to travel aboard the ROYAL SOVEREIGN but on board the yacht ROYAL GEORGE, built some thirteen years later than the former, in 1817. The ROYAL SOVEREIGN ended her duties as a Royal yacht in 1832. She was one of the direct casualties of the radical politician Joseph Hume (1777-1855). Hume appointed himself guardian of the public purse and challenged every single item of public expenditure. He

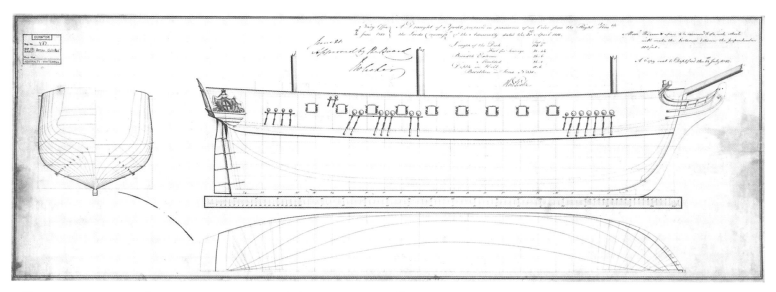

The ROYAL GEORGE enabled George IV to visit Scotland in 1822, the first monarch to do so since Charles II. The yacht performed the same service for Queen Victoria in 1842 behind a tug. (National Maritime Museum)

questioned the need for five Royal yachts and won his point, for ROYAL SOVEREIGN and WILLIAM & MARY were pensioned off as depot ships and the ROYAL CHARLOTTE sent away to be broken up.

However, the ROYAL GEORGE enabled George IV to visit Scotland in 1822, the first British Monarch to do so since Charles II. It was fitting, therefore, that a Royal yacht should be the conveyance.

Charles would not have approved of the way the ROYAL GEORGE reached Leith, for she was towed there by a steamer. Boteler heralds this new method of progression by remarking that 'the measured strokes of the paddle wheels were a new and most peculiar sound to us'.

The ROYAL GEORGE was a magnificent yacht, designed to suit the mood and convenience of the Prince Regent. Commander Gavin in 'Royal Yachts' observes that 'one can trace the ideas and taste of the creator of the Royal Pavilion in the ornamentation proposed for the ROYAL GEORGE.' A contemporary description reinforces her suitability. 'The vessel is the most elegant ever seen. The cabin doors are of mahogany, with gilt mouldings, and the windows of plate glass. Ornamental devices in abundance are placed in various parts, all highly gilt, and producing a superb appearance.'

Such magnificence ornamented a strong and useful hull, for the ROYAL GEORGE served four sovereigns and was in commission for 88 years. She was finally broken up in 1905. From 1843 to 1901 the yacht had been employed as an accommodation vessel, hulk seems the wrong word, for officers and men of the Royal Yachts.

ROYAL GEORGE changed the face of royal yachting. Her last official engagement had been in 1842 when Queen Victoria made her one and only passage in the vessel to Leith, a distance of just over 400 nautical miles. The Queen noticed with a certain displeasure that the six knots procession of tug, yacht and escort was often overtaken by steam ships. Her Majesty's diary for 1842 records: *'Tuesday, August 30.*

> We heard, to our great distress, that we had only gone 58 miles since eight o'clock last night. How annoying and provoking this is! We remained on deck all day lying on sofas; the sea was very rough towards evening, and I was very ill. We reached *Flamborough Head* on the Yorkshire coast by half-past five.'

Royal yachts found themselves in peculiar places. The Prince of Wales' frigate is seen on the Serpentine. (Parker Gallery)

The Prime Minister, Sir Robert Peel, was no doubt told, for after the Queen returned from Scotland aboard the hired 1,000 ton paddle steamer TRIDENT, he assured her that a steam vessel would be available next year 'suitable in every respect for Your Majesty's accommodation'.

So ended state occasions under sail. The Royal Family had not, however, turned their back on the wind, for the Duke of Cumberland had ordered a splendid miniature frigate of 50 tons for Virginia Water. She was built like a Windermere steamer, and carried in sections to the Water, to be assembled there in 1833. ROYAL ADELAIDE, as she was known, was enjoyed by William IV; she was named after his Queen, but was broken up in 1877. Virginia Water had a certain charm for the Royal Family, as Edward VII built and converted in 1904 a 42′ cutter into a 10 gun brig for the use of the Royal children on that lake. She was known as THE BRIG and was broken up in 1919. The guns from the ROYAL ADELAIDE are still in use today, as a battery of signal cannons in front of the Royal Yacht Squadron at Cowes

Edward VII returned to sail with BRITANNIA, perhaps the most successful of all the Royal yachts and she carried on that tradition under George V. The BRITANNIA is described in some detail in Chapter III.

But to return to Victoria and the advent of the Royal Steam Yacht. Sir Robert Peel was as good as his promise, for the keel of the VICTORIA & ALBERT was laid on November 9th 1842, on the anniversary of the birth of the Prince of Wales. She was launched six months later, at Pembroke, on April 26th, 1843 by the Countess of Cawdor. Lady Cawdor had better fortune in this ceremony than Prince Albert when he launched the Brunel steamer GREAT BRITAIN from her building dock at Bristol three months later. His discomfort and remarkable recovery is recorded in the *Illustrated London News* for July 29th, 1843.

'As the immense structure of iron floated on the water, the Prince broke against the bows of the ship a bottle of wine, and pronounced as the name by which the vessel is after to be known, the words "THE GREAT BRITAIN". The hawser by which the steam ship was attached to the Avon steamer, however, broke; and the first bottle thrown by the Prince, fell 10′ short of the vessel, which, in being warped out by a larger hawser attached to her, veered towards the Royal Pavilion. Another bottle of champagne was handed to His Royal Highness, who threw it at the vessel; it struck her bows, and the broken glass and the wine fell upon the heads of the persons below, who were shoving against her sides, and assisting to keep her clear of the walls of the dock. This, the crowning point of the occasion, took place at a quarter past three.'

The Queen's first voyage on the VICTORIA & ALBERT had its moments, too. The weather, as reported by the *Illustrated London News* 'did not augur a very promising appearance, being dark and lowering, with the Scotch mist falling, that would wet an Englishman to the skin'. The weather encouraged the Mayor and Aldermen to strip off their robes of office for the benefit of Her Majesty. Mr Warren, the Mate, had an embarrassing time, too, for he fell off the accommodation ladder as Her Majesty was leaving the yacht at Ryde, though he was soon recovered, unhurt.

VICTORIA & ALBERT made her way down Channel as far as Falmouth and then across to the French coast, where King Louis Philippe met the Queen at Tréport. They returned to England, landing at Brighton. On the way, an amusing occurrence took place. Her Majesty settled with Lady Canning and Lady Bloomfield behind one of the paddle boxes out of the wind. After a little while they noticed the crew were gathering together in little groups and

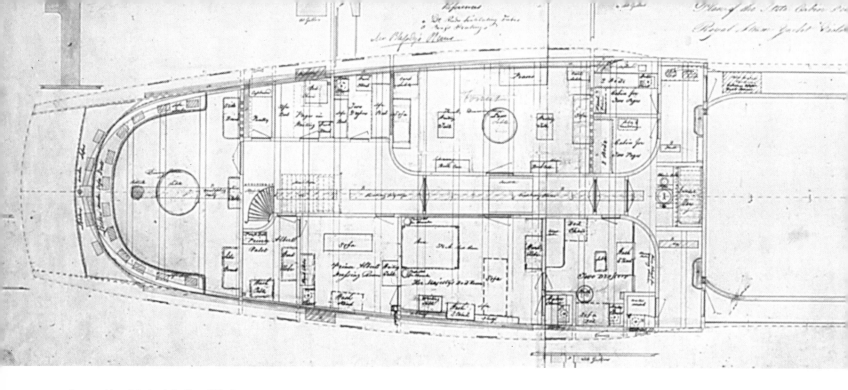

whispering. The Queen thought there might be a mutiny in the offing and summoned Lord Adolphus Fitz-Clarence. Lord Adolphus discovered that the crew were embarrassed by the fact that Her Majesty had sat tight up against the grog store so they were denied their usual refreshment. On hearing this the Queen said she would leave the shelter of the paddle box, provided that she, too, could have a glass of grog. When it was brought to her she made a remark recorded in 'The Victorian Empire' by James Taylor. 'I'm afraid I can only make the same remark I did once before, that I think it would be very good if it were stronger.' The Royal reply delighted the crew.

The paddle driven VICTORIA & ALBERT was considerably larger than her predecessors, being 225′ overall, over 100′ longer than the ROYAL GEORGE. She was, therefore, not suitable for all ports the Queen wished to visit and so the propeller driven FAIRY was commissioned in 1844 as a tender. Four years later a further yacht, a paddler, ELPHIN, was built at Chatham, of mahogany, on the double diagonal principle, as was employed with the first VICTORIA & ALBERT. Although ELPHIN was described as a tender to the larger yacht, she had a particular purpose, that of serving the Queen at her new house at Osborne, near Cowes, on the Isle of Wight.

Victoria had stayed at Norris Castle, just south of Osborne, in 1833. On marrying Prince Albert three years later, they both decided they wanted a private house and were keen that it should be paid for by them, rather than by the Commissioner of Works & Forests. They considered Eaglehurst, near Calshot, on the mainland, but it was too small and in 1845 they settled on the large, rather stark, 18th century house, Osborne. Prince Albert, with his usual verve and imagination, together with the builder, Thomas Cubitt, created the remarkable Italianate villa that was to become their favourite home.

ELPHIN acted as the taxi on what became known as the 'milk run', carrying the Queen's messenger, despatches and no doubt serving the house and estate as well. FAIRY was the Queen's conveyance to the Island. She was later replaced by ALBERTA, a paddle wheel yacht capable of 14 knots, built in 1863.

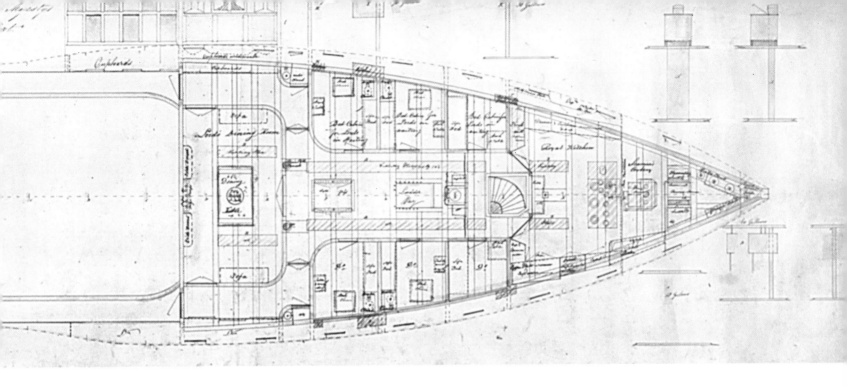

The old VICTORIA & ALBERT was succeeded in 1855 by the second of the same name. Only 12 years had passed since the first of Victoria's yachts had been launched, but she was already too small and too slow for the Queen's requirements. The furthest the old yacht had voyaged was to Gibraltar and then without royalty aboard. She was, however, used as an escort to the new yacht and was renamed OSBORNE in honour of their delight. The OSBORNE, ex VICTORIA & ALBERT I, was eventually broken up in 1868 and the name OSBORNE passed to another yacht built in 1874, serving as a tender to the principal Royal Yacht until 1908. OSBORNE II was a favourite of the Prince and Princess of Wales and they enjoyed many a cruise in her, sometimes in the Mediterranean, in the 70's, 80's and 90's of the last century.

VICTORIA & ALBERT II had some curious features. The upper deck was not scrubbed teak but covered with a new patent material – linoleum – over which, perhaps mercifully, a carpet was laid when the Queen was aboard. There were two tea houses there, too. Below, the cabins were covered in box pleated rosebud chintz. The doors were of fashionable birds eye 'maple' with ivory handles and, in 1888, the yacht was lit with electric light, superceding candles.

It was perhaps surprising that paddle wheel propulsion was again chosen and there was criticism that the newly developed propeller had not been adopted. After all, Brunel had proven the screw following the launch of the GREAT BRITAIN in 1843, and a year later the celebrated test of strength between paddle and screw had been demonstrated with a thoroughness that only Victorians would have attempted. This was the tug-o-war between the two thousand ton vessels of identical hull shape, built especially for the purpose, with engines of the same power and manufacture. ALECTO was driven by paddle and RATTLER by screw. RATTLER won hands down. Why then was the Royal yacht equipped with paddles? It may have been that the Queen liked 'the measured strokes of the paddle wheels' referred to by Captain Boteler when he first heard them. Dr McGowan quotes a more informed source, the words of Commander Crispin, Captain of the first VICTORIA &

A Royal steam tender. (Beken of Cowes)

ALBERT in the National Maritime Museum booklet 'Royal Yachts'. 'I am convinced till further improvement shall have much lessened, or entirely removed the shock and vibration arising from the screw itself – a screw ship as a yacht will in that vital and all important point – the personal comfort of her Majesty, prove a total failure'. Certainly the paddle steamer commands a following even today, as witnessed by the recent restoration and popularity of the Clyde Steamer WAVERLEY.

This liking, however, was not shared by one of the Empress of Austria's attendants who went with her mistress to Madeira when Queen Victoria kindly lent the yacht to Her Imperial Highness in 1860. Commander Gavin records the letter in full, but extracts paint a picture of the less pleasurable side that can mar even a Royal excursion in a yacht 360′ long.

'Each moment a wave dashed like a cannon-ball in my place and then quickly over the deck; in the intervals was heard the shrill sound of the boatswain's whistle, the increasing signals of the commander, the running and cries of the sailors, then a frightful crash, which, now I thought, is the moment when we shall all be buried in the deep sea. Suddenly our ship sustained a more violent shock than ever. I was thrown from my bed, which quickly followed me, but by great fortune it was stopped by a firm and well-secured table, or else my leg and arm must have been broken; everything about the Empress was scattered about, looking-glass, china broken, her watch thrown from her bed, chairs, tables, nothing escaped in Her Majesty's cabin nor in ours—the most useful and necessary utensils broken into a thousand pieces—in the kitchen all was ruin, the whole service of the Queen, glasses, pitchers, all was clatter and confusion, the terror of the people arose to the highest pitch, for the sailors fell from the masts, broken legs, dislocations, sprains, were the consequence; on the next morning it was discovered there was a rent in the side of the ship nearest to the stairs leading to the wheels.

'The self-possession and composure of the captain, the Hon. Captain Denman, was admirable and marvellous; as often as he could he came below to us to console and comfort us, which he did so successfully that we had no more anxiety, but were calm.

'Through all, the Empress and Princess Windischgratz were well; Her Majesty was, however, obliged to lie down directly she came to her cabin; to walk was impossible, we were thrown from one side to another; from the beginning of Saturday we did not eat a morsel, although we were always being persuaded to try and eat, for we were told our sufferings would be greater on a fasting stomach. But it was literally impossible for us to eat anything. On Sunday evening I had a small piece of tongue—Monday nothing—Tuesday a little ham, and it was only on Wednesday that I could take some cold beef, cheese, and bread.'

After Albert's death in 1861, the Queen confined herself principally to the waters of the British Isles. The yacht, though, continued her state duties and in 1896 was secured below the Nicholas Bridge that crosses the Neva in St. Petersburg, with the Duke and Duchess of Connaught aboard, to attend the Czar's coronation.

The 90's contained brilliant days, perhaps the most celebrated in the annals of yachting. No doubt, at the time, they looked without end, a period of calm, sparkling and gilded years stretching to a bright horizon like a glorious summer's day at sea. The Queen symbolised the mood, for she was the apex and the rock on which all this was built. Her yacht VICTORIA & ALBERT II steaming through the fleet at the Diamond Jubilee Review of 1897 epitomised this. There were five lines of warships, four of them were British. The fleet was made up of 21 battleships, 12 first class cruisers, 27 second class cruisers and innumerable destroyers and lesser craft, making a grand total of 155 ships. The Queen was

78 Passage de Prince de Galles à Port-Saïd.

The Royal Yacht VICTORIA & ALBERT II at Port Said. (Radio Times Hulton Picture Library)

too infirm to be there but, no doubt, looked on from the windows of Osborne. The Royal yacht was a true palace afloat, carrying the Prince and Princess of Wales, the Empress of Germany and representatives of all the royal houses of Europe. No Royal Review before or since created such a spectacle. The Royal Navy provided glorious might and C.A. Parsons (later Sir Charles Parsons) provided, unofficially, the inventive spirit of the age, the turbine powered TURBINIA, racing through the fleet at 34 knots.

It was left to the most beautiful of all Victoria's yachts, ALBERTA, to provide the final wake. Her Majesty Queen Victoria passed away on January 22nd, 1901 and ALBERTA, perhaps named after Princess Louise Caroline Alberta, Duchess of Argyll, took her from her beloved Osborne to the mainland and from there she was carried to her last resting place at Frogmore, Windsor. Life afloat and ashore would never be quite the same again.

The Queen had loved her second VICTORIA & ALBERT. The softening of ornament between the first V. & A. and the next had been Prince Albert's idea and after his death the Queen would not change a thing of his doing. The simplicity of the chintz linings was his and such a light touch stood out amongst the heavy, ornate, but beautifully made furniture and rich decoration of the Victorian Gothick. Contemporary yachts, outside the Royal fleet, described later, emphasise this difference in marine furnishing.

Before Victoria died, the Government was again determined to give the Queen a yacht that could play a suitable role in her vast Empire and so VICTORIA & ALBERT III was planned. Her Majesty was lukewarm about the idea and, in fact, never set foot on the yacht. She was particularly sad at the thought of parting with her favourite, VICTORIA & ALBERT II.

The Royal Yacht ALBERTA, *the most beautiful of Queen Victoria's fleet.*

The household dining cabin of the VICTORIA & ALBERT III *was right aft and conformed to the shape of the stern. The upholstery was in crimson morocco.* (John White)

However, plans for the new yacht went ahead and though 80′ longer, she was to be as like her predecessor as possible, both inside and outside, using or copying most of the fittings of VICTORIA & ALBERT II. The same light touch and lack of ostentation, following Albert's example, was to be the keynote to her internal design. At first the plan was to call her 'Windsor Castle', following the tradition of the Royal Yacht OSBORNE, in selecting another Royal residence. The Queen favoured 'Balmoral', not wishing to mar happy memories by following VICTORIA & ALBERT with a 'III', but finally the 'III' was decided upon. The Queen's only other worry, when consulted over design, was about bumping her head when being carried on the stairway in her chair. This was overcome by providing a lift, perhaps one of the first in any yacht.

The Queen's final disenchantment with her new vessel came nine months after launching by the Duchess of York in May 1899. The engines and masts were being fitted and the yacht was about to be taken out of the dock when she began to list alarmingly to starboard – 20 degrees were recorded before the tide left her stranded like a particularly beautiful whale, jammed between the blocks at the bottom of the dock and the dock side.

Sir William White, Director of Naval Construction and the Corps of Naval Constructors, came in for severe criticism. The Goschen Committee was quickly set up to look into her design and try to discover what had gone wrong. They reported that Sir William's work was good and that he had designed a sea-kindly vessel but when the yacht was fitted out, so much had been piled aboard and such heavy materials had been used, without the necessary thought or care, that his calculations were upset and so, inevitably, was the yacht.

The dockyard set about lightening her and adding ballast to her double bottom. The enquiry and careful study ensured that she was one of the best examined and tested yachts afloat but 'Old Salts' were not convinced and longshoremen and seamen who had not served on her, shook their heads and muttered that 'she'd roll over' one day. Nonsense, of course, but wholesome gossip for the quayside. (Author's note: I went aboard her in 1937 as a child of five and can remember my mother saying that she was unstable, as though we had better step gently for fear of a catastrophe in Cowes Roads.)

*Princess Victoria's stateroom aboard
VICTORIA & ALBERT III was decorated in
rosebud chintz.* (John White)

*The state dining cabin aboard VICTORIA &
ALBERT III. The tables would seat forty-four.
There were three fine Teheran carpets, the
curtains were of silk and the chairs and
settees were covered in blue morocco.*
(John White)

*The twin companion-way to the upper deck
of VICTORIA & ALBERT III was semi-circular in
form, in Georgian style and decorated in
white and gold.* (John White)

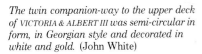

VICTORIA & ALBERT III was in every sense magnificent and in the fine tradition of her predecessors. Her interior is well illustrated in the photographic record, but a word about her other intimate details.

The propeller had finally won the day and by the 90's the only paddlers were Admiralty tugs, ferries and pleasure steamers. VICTORIA & ALBERT was twin screw and originally was to have three bell-topped funnels, but two were finally decided upon to relieve her 18 Belleville boilers. The engines were vertical triple expansion, built by Humphreys & Tennant & Co. They developed 11,000 I.H.P., giving her a speed of 20 knots, five knots more than the former yacht. The triple expansion engine almost cured one of the difficulties in the quest for quiet and seemingly effortless travel, by eliminating vibration.

The new yacht's construction was novel for she had a steel hull, sheathed in wood. The designers wished her to look like a yacht rather than a commercial vessel and the planking would certainly achieve this while at the same time helping to insulate the crew and passengers against both heat and cold.

The new VICTORIA & ALBERT began her career by taking King Edward and Queen Alexandra to Flushing. Queen Alexandra's Pekinese had a narrow escape before they left Cowes, for the little dog fell overboard during a visit to RRS DISCOVERY, just launched. The VICTORIA & ALBERT cruised down to Gibraltar showing off her paces as the world's finest steam yacht to the King of Portugal, who was a keen yachtsman and owner of the steam yacht AMELIA II. Her successor, the ram bowed AMELIA III, built in 1901 under the name BANSHEE was bought from Colonel Harry MacCalmont in 1905. The Colonel, a great horseman whose horse Isinglass made him £55,000 in one season, was an enthusiastic yachtsman. He seemed to make a habit of selling his old yachts to royalty, for his superb GIRALDA, built in 1894, was one of the first British yachts to exceed 1,000 tons. She became the Spanish Royal Yacht in 1898. GIRALDA often carried King Alphonso XIII to Cowes, where he raced his 15 metre HISPANIA.

King Edward had just performed a sad duty, that of ordering his mother's favourite yacht, VICTORIA & ALBERT II, to be broken up and burnt. He tried to reprieve her at the last minute, for his coronation review, but it proved too expensive a tribute.

The King remembered the sad duty that ALBERTA had performed by carrying his mother's remains across the Solent and Spithead by placing a memorial plate on her deck which read:

> 'V.R. I Here rested the beloved remains of Queen Victoria from February lst to 2nd, 1901. Born May 24th, 1819. Died January 22nd, 1901.'

VICTORIA & ALBERT steamed 100,791 nautical miles from her launch to the outbreak of the First War and although this book concludes at the beginning of that catastrophe a glimpse into the future shows that the third V. & A., which by then was some 36 years old, was withdrawn from service in 1937 and broken up soon after the Second War. The first VICTORIA & ALBERT (later OSBORNE) served the country for 16 years and VICTORIA & ALBERT II for 46 years.

King Edward decided that OSBORNE should be retired and she was paid off in 1908. There was, however a requirement for a smaller yacht, as his mother had discovered before him, and so a half-size version of VICTORIA & ALBERT was commissioned and named ALEXANDRA after the Queen. She was launched by Princess Louise, Duchess of Argyll, whose last Christian name had inspired ALBERTA. Again propeller driven, the

The Royal Yacht ALBERTA taking the remains of Queen Victoria from Cowes to Portsmouth in 1901. VICTORIA & ALBERT III takes station astern. (Cadland Archives)

yacht benefited from TURBINIA's rush through the fleet at the Review of 1897 and was powered by two Parsons turbines, fed by three Yarrow boilers which gave her a speed of just under 19 knots. She was a beautiful ship but served only 17 years, a year longer than the first VICTORIA & ALBERT, before being sold and converted into a Norwegian cruise liner.

ALBERTA continued in service until March 30th, 1912, before meeting her end at the shipbreakers in 1913, a service of 51 years. The little ALBERTA lasted longer than her larger sisters. This was fitting for she was the most beautiful steam yacht ever built.

Queen Victoria and King Edward were not the only monarchs to enjoy and benefit from the yacht. Maritime monarchial magnificence was seen all around Europe and the harbours of the Mediterranean were often hosts to these vessels. The following short survey does not pretend to be exhaustive, but rather more an album of the more remarkable and amusing aspects.

Imperial Russia

LIVADIA, a yacht built for Czar Alexander II as a floating palace by the British builders, John Elder & Co., was certainly that. Her claim to attention is well merited for LIVADIA was nearly circular, having an overall length of 235′, a beam of 153′ and a draught of 6′ 6″. Her underwater shape resembled a turbot and the whole concept was to prevent her rolling. The idea had been tried by the Russians in their warships and the design was reasonably successful.

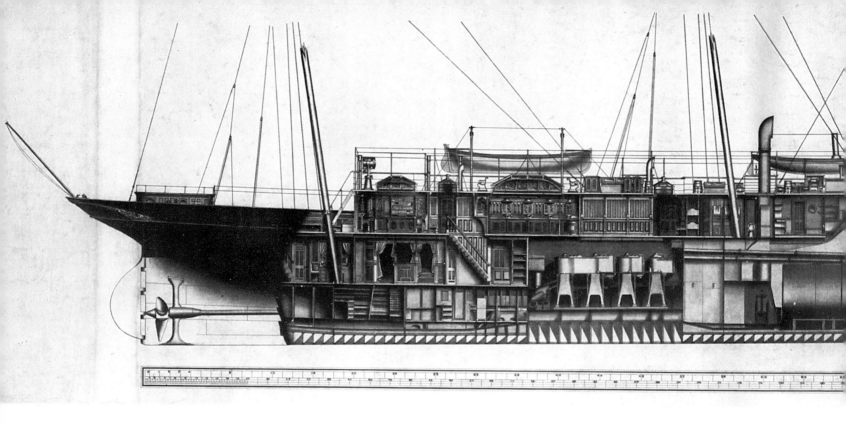

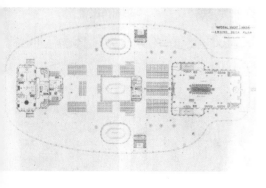

Cutaway drawing of the Spanish Royal Yacht GIRALDA, originally built for Col. Harry McCalmont in 1894, was one of the first British yachts to exceed 1,000 tons. (National Maritime Museum)

The Imperial Russian yacht LIVADIA, built for Alexander II by John Elder and Company of Govan in 1880. Her turbot-shaped hull had an overall length of 235 feet and an astonishingly wide beam of 153 feet. (National Maritime Museum)

Alexander III, who succeeded after his father's assassination in 1881, built a more conventional yacht, POLIARNAIA ZVESDA, at St. Petersburg in 1888. Pole Star, as her name translated, followed the convention of having three masts in the manner of the British Royal yachts.

LIVADIA had five, two pairs and a central main mast amidships. STANDART, built in 1895, was perhaps the best known of the Russian royal yachts after LIVADIA. She, too, was a three-master, and again the purpose of the rig was to fly flags.

STANDART had the glazed, square ports that were a feature of all the VICTORIA & ALBERTs. These were inherited from the working gun ports of the wooden walls and, in particular, ROYAL GEORGE. The similarities did not end there, as can be seen by comparing dimensions. BRITANNIA is put in as a comparison with today (1979).

NAME	VICTORIA & ALBERT III	STANDART	HOHENZOLLERN	MAHROUSSA	BRITANNIA
BUILT	1899	1895	1893	1865	1954
L.O.A. (ft.)	422.2	420	382.6	420.2 (1905)*	412.2
L.W.L. (ft.)	380.1	370	375	370	381
Beam (ft.)	50.3	50.5	45.9	42.2	55.1
Draught (ft.)	17	20.5	23.1	17.5	15.6
Tonnage	5,505 (T.M.)	4,334 (T.M.)	3,773 (T.M.)	3,581 (T.M.)	5,111 (T.M.)
I.H.P.	11,000	11,640	9,500	6,560 (Orig. 1,600)	12,000 (B.H.P.)
Speed (Knots)	20	18	21.5	15 (Orig. 11)	22.75

* Twice lengthened in 1872 and 1905

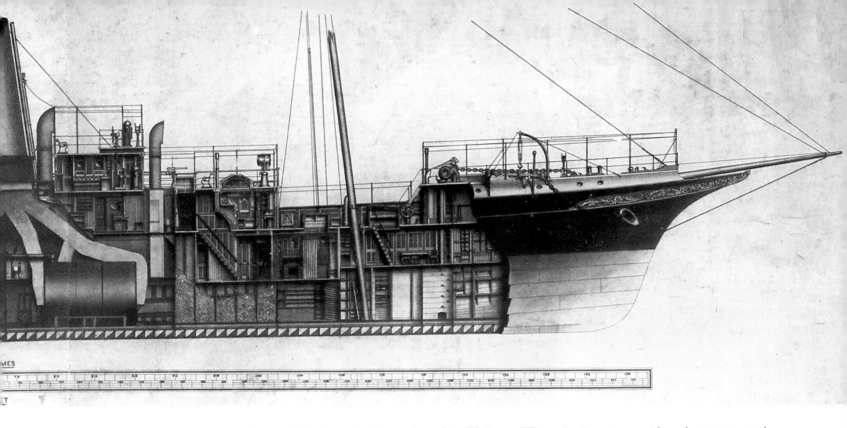

MES

T

*The aggressive bow of the Kaiser's yacht
HOHENZOLLERN contrasted significantly
with most steam yachts of the period.*
(Beken of Cowes)

It is difficult to believe that Sir William White had not considered STANDART's advantages before putting his own plans for an ideal Royal yacht to Queen Victoria. Equally, Burmeister & Wain, of Copenhagen, who built the Czar's yacht, no doubt had a look at the highly successful but smaller VICTORIA & ALBERT II.

The Russian funnels had not the bell mouth eloquence of Queen Victoria's yachts where they were certainly sensitive additions.

The Russians also felt it necessary to paint the funnel tops black, no doubt to save sooting, which was not a requirement in the British Royal yachts. Such problems were no doubt looked after by careful stoking and naval pride. VICTORIA & ALBERT looked less ponderous and enjoyed sweeter lines because her deckhouses were painted white and so were lost to the eye.

STANDART witnessed the end of Imperial Russia and was taken over by the Soviet Navy, serving as a mine layer, amongst other duties, under the name MARTI until 1963, a remarkable span of 68 years.

Imperial Germany

The Kaiser, on the other hand, had different ideas. As Queen Victoria's grandson and with the Prince of Wales as his uncle he understood the need for a Royal yacht, and from the latter he gained an enthusiasm for sailing. He forwarded both; the first in 1875 with the KAISER ADLER, an iron paddler of 268′ overall and then the GRILLE of 160′, built a few years later as a Baltic yacht. He soon realised that he needed something more impressive than these and so HOHENZOLLERN was conceived and built at Stettin by the Vulcan Yard in 1893.

The profile of HOHENZOLLERN was completely different to that of other royal yachts. The Kaiser employed the naval ram bow and the cruiser stern. This aggressive look was

The Imperial Russian yacht STANDART built in 1895 was often seen at Cowes. Her rig was designed to fly flags. (Beken of Cowes)

The Imperial German paddle yacht KAISER ADLER built in 1875. (Beken of Cowes)

significant, for the Kaiser saw the yacht as an important part of the Imperial German Navy. The square ports of the VICTORIA & ALBERT and STANDART decorated her hull. The funnels were those developed for the KAISER ADLER with a recessed bell sprouting from a wider casing.

HOHENZOLLERN was often at Cowes and, indeed, attended the procession of ALBERTA, VICTORIA & ALBERT and OSBORNE in front of the Admiralty yacht ENCHANTRESS at the funeral of Queen Victoria. She often attended Cowes Week and part of her function was to act as a tender to the Kaiser's racing yachts METEORS I-V. METEOR IV, constructed at Kiel in 1909 by Germania Werst to the designs of Max Oerst, was one of the most beautiful racing yachts ever built. The Kaiser's enthusiasm for sailing turned the German people to the sea for pleasure as well as war.

A very much grander design was begun just before the First War. Construction was interrupted by hostilities and the new yacht was never completed. She would have been more than 500′ overall, nearly 100′ longer than the VICTORIA & ALBERT III, and her design displacement was 7,300 tons. In profile, the new HOHENZOLLERN was a classical steam yacht of her period, with a clipper bow and a counter stern. The new yacht would have been the largest in the world, but the war put an end to that ambition, along with all the Emperor's other dreams.

Opposite
METEOR IV racing off Osborne Bay in 1911. The Kaiser's racing flag, a red eagle on a white ground, is worn on the main. (Beken of Cowes)

The research yacht PRINCESSE ALICE II built for Prince Albert of Monaco in 1898 cruised as far north as Spitzbergen and Jan Mayen Island. (Steele collection)

The Principality of Monaco

His Serene Highness Prince Albert of Monaco employed his yacht to improve man's understanding of the deep. He served in the Spanish Navy, and having become keen on the animals and plants under the sea and the physical environment in which they lived, he used his yachts for oceanographic research. The first of these was the schooner HIRONDELLE, which was soon to prove too small, and so the first PRINCESSE ALICE was built in 1891 to replace her. Unlike other principal royal yachts of the latter part of the 19th century, she was rigged as a three masted topsail schooner and was built on the banks of the London river by Richard Green. Her auxiliary steam engine was made by Messrs. Penn and Sons, who were responsible for the engines of the Royal yachts FAIRY (1845), ALBERTA (1863) and VICTORIA & ALBERT II (1855).

In the six years that folllowed, from 1891 to 1897, the Prince completed six important expeditions. He managed to sink his net 5,530 metres in the Monaco trench off Madeira as part of a study of deep sea fauna, and PRINCESSE ALICE's steam winches improved the hauling speed of the nets. The Prince was well aware of the problems of hand hauling from his experiences aboard HIRONDELLE. Bringing back a net from 3,000 metres then took some 13 hours, Albert playing his full part. Excited by Arctic waters and after 13 years of research, the Prince of Monaco commissioned a new yacht, the 1,400 ton PRINCESSE ALICE II, in 1898. She was strengthened for ice, equipped with the most modern oceanographic equipment and cruised as far north as Spitzbergen and Jan Mayen Island.

His last yacht, the HIRONDELLE II, of 1,600 tons, built in 1911, was capable of 15 knots.

PRINCESSE ALICE II decorates the badge of the famous Museum of Oceanography above Monte-Carlo. (Musée Oceanographique, Monaco)

Prince Albert called two of his yachts HIRONDELLE or 'Swallow' because he admired the little bird for its 'adventurous resolution and an elegant modesty and fine plumage'. It was not a bad description too, for this remarkable man.

France, Egypt, Sir John Burgoyne & The Sun King

Napoleon III was a yachtsman of some pretensions. He proclaimed himself Emperor in 1852 and by 1858 had taken delivery of the schooner rigged paddle yacht L'AIGLE. One of her most celebrated duties was to attend the opening of the Suez Canal with the Empress Eugénie aboard. However, looking back at the event, it is not L'AIGLE that is remembered among the yachts then present, but the Egyptian Royal Yacht MAHROUSSA, built by Samuda Bros., Poplar, London in 1865, two years after Victoria's ALBERTA, for she is still serving the Egyptian government today (see table of dimensions, page 32).

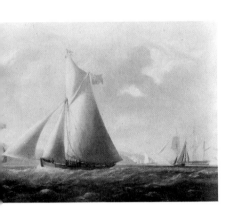

The cutter GAZELLE owned by Sir John Burgoyne rescued Napoleon III's Empress, Eugénie and carried her from Deauville to Cowes in 1870. (National Maritime Museum)

However, to return to the French Emperor. He had a series of yachts, usually conversions, including the screw barquentine JEROME NAPOLEON, built in the 1850's and LA REINE HORTENSE, also 1850 vintage, the last royal yacht of France. Napoleon came to Cowes and was elected a member of the Royal Yacht Squadron. His picture, presented by him, commanded the Library in the Castle and stretched from floor to ceiling, until redecoration in the 1960's saw its removal and sale. His wife Eugénie, though, had reason to be grateful to the Club for immediately after the Emperor's fall from power, she sought refuge and escape aboard the Squadron cutter GAZELLE, owned by Sir John Burgoyne, who was sheltering in Deauville, awaiting more moderate conditions for the passage home. The arrival of the Empress persuaded him to forsake comfort and on September 2nd, 1870 he set sail for Cowes. This experience encouraged her enthusiasm for the sea, for after Napoleon's death she became the owner of the steam yacht THISTLE.

The Sun King, Louis XIV, 200 years before had brought saltwater ships, or at least models of them, to the fresh water of 'Le Grande Canal' at his Palace of Versailles. He imported oared vessels, gondolas and miniature frigates. Charles II was intrigued, as might be imagined, and he gave King Louis a yacht for his growing collection. Built on the Thames, this ornamental garden conceit was sailed over on its own bottom. The magnificent marine spectacle was often imitated on a much smaller scale in England by lesser folk. Children and parsons sailed their models on ornamental ponds and elderly mariners forsook the salt-water and disturbed the ducks by firing broadsides at them from diminutive replicas of their last commands.

Charles II, set an example that was followed, not only by his own heirs and successors, but by the royal heads of Europe. The salt-water palace was not, however, the exclusive toy or tool of royalty, for their subjects developed the idea for their own pleasure or profit. Men of like mind banded together, inspired by the royal example, and the yacht club came into its own.

CHAPTER II
The Yacht Club

The Club-house

At first thought it may seem strange for yachtsmen to band together at all to form a club, particularly when it means responsibility for bricks and mortar. The hallmark of the sailor, particularly those who cruise, is independence from the land and the ability to go where wind or fancy wills.

The Irish were appropriately the first to see that boats afloat and a room for celebration ashore provided a way of increasing enjoyment. Water was all very well but something added was an improvement.

The ingenious ideas of Sir William Petty, already described, show the independence of thought and power of invention that existed in Ireland in the late 17th and early 18th centuries. By 1720, the waters of Cork Harbour had proven so productive to the sport and pastime of sailing that the Water Club of the Harbour of Cork blossomed in that year. The organisers drew up rules and saw the merit in limiting the club, first to six and then to 25 members. Indeed, they were even more insular, for the 'secretary' was to be dismissed if he permitted strangers in the club-room, except on special occasions. This room is said to have been on Hawlbowline Island, an appropriate name for the home of the first yacht club. The secretary was called the 'Knight of the Island' and he arranged the fortnightly sails and dinners to coincide with the spring tide. Each member took it in turn to entertain his fellows and excess expense and behaviour were controlled by limiting the number of bottles of wine to one a head – unless someone talked of sailing after dinner, in which case, he was fined a 'bumper' of wine. Whether this was for immediate consumption and a method of contravening the rules is not revealed.

When not at the table, the members were energetic at sea. They neither cruised nor raced but manoeuvred under the command of their Admiral, who wore, in company with Admirals of the Fleet of the Royal Navy, a particularly large Union Jack at the masthead, though with a harp at its centre, a privilege officially and uniquely granted to the Admiral of the Club in 1759.

A quotation from 'A Tour Through Ireland', printed by J. Roberts, Warwick Lane, London in 1748, gives an insight into a day at sea with the Water Club.

> 'It is somewhat like that of the Doge of Venice wedding the sea. A set of worthy gentlemen who have formed themselves into a body, which they call "The Water Club", proceed a few leagues out to sea once a year, in a number of little vessels, which for painting and gilding exceed the King's yacht at Greenwich and Deptford. Their Admiral, who is elected annually, and hoists his flag on board his little vessel, leads the van and receives the honours of the flag. The rest of the fleet fall in their proper stations and keep their line in the same manner as the King's ships. This fleet is attended with a prodigious number of boats, which, with their colours flying, drums beating and trumpets sounding, forms one of the most agreeable and splendid sights your Lordships can conceive.'

Naval discipline was the order of the day and members were made well aware of it. The sailing club laid down the law about behaviour at sea. Members were instructed that if they wished to land a sick man, they had to signal in a particular way for the Admiral's

The Castle of the Royal Yacht Squadron. The tower on the west end was likened to 'the fumes of the cook's stock pot – a perfect olla podrida – a mixture of everything'. (Beken of Cowes)

Lord Anglesey's PEARL, *the Hon. C.A. Pelham's* FALCON *and Lord Belfast's* WATERWITCH *off the Warner, painted by W.J. Huggins.* (Royal Yacht Squadron)

permission. If the Admiral showed a red, rather than a white flag in the shrouds and fired a gun, permission was refused and the sick man had to stay where he was.

Disputes within the Club were dealt with under Rule XXI, which read:

> 'That the Admiral singly or any three captains whom he shall appoint, do decide all controversies and disputes that may arise in the Club, and any captain that shall refuse to abide by such decision is to be expelled. NB: This order to extend to the Chaplain, or any other inferior officers.'

Whether this rule was strong enough, or that the Church took exception to the Chaplain being referred to in such terms, is mere speculation, but the Club went into decline after 1765 until revived by a new set of 'original members' in 1806. These included the Marquess of Thomond, Lord Kingsale, the Fitz-Geralds, Penroses and Newenhams. Robert Newenham had been Secretary in 1760.

Colonel John Bateman Fitz-Gerald, the Knight of Glin, was a celebrated Irish yachtsman of that period. Though Colonel of both the Royal Glin Artillery and Hussars, he was keen on the sea. He built both the bow-fronted Glin Castle on the south side of the River Shannon and the yacht FARMER in the 1780's. She took her name from the Irish Captain of His Majesty's ship QUEBEC that conquered the French frigate SURVEILLANTE in October, 1779, only to catch fire when her mainmast fell to the deck. The Knight used to sail his 18 gun cutter up and down the West Coast, his volunteer band playing the Gaelic ballad 'In Praise of the Knight's Boat FARMER' written about the yacht, which begins by praising the martial capabilities of the vessel:

> 'Indeed she would let shots fly with vigour and Gibraltar would be taken if she entered the Straits.'

The song continues and describes life aboard:

> 'You should see the FARMER leaving her anchorage
> From sweet lovely Glin, laden with gentry on a
> Hard March morning with the wind from the north-west
> And my prayer to (St.) Senan for fair weather,
> Her crew and company in high spirits aboard.
> Gerald (brother) and the Knight gaming and drinking
> Murray providing the music............
> And her timbers grew in lovely pleasant Glin
> And may the King of Grace favour her wherever she goes'.

> (By Maurice Kerins, National Library of Ireland 6494(83)
> Translated by Padraig de Brun of the Institute of Advanced Studies, Dublin)

The Knight sold FARMER in 1803. His son owned the cutter REINVELLE seen racing against PAUL PRY for a wager of £50.

Although no doubt the in-built hospitality continued at Cork, the Water Club directed attention towards organising regattas for local people. Enthusiasm drained away again until 1828, when they joined forces with the Monkstown Club and the Cork Yacht Club. Later the Royal Cork, was founded, the first yacht club and shore base to be founded in the British Isles.

The story of the Royal Cork certainly illustrates that sailing and the joys of the table ashore go together and this partnership was to develop so that bricks and mortar and the yacht afloat became truly wedded. This development was slow, but by the second half of

The Knight of Glin's cutter REINVELLE racing against another Irish yacht PAUL PRY was for a wager of £50. (The Knight of Glin)

the 19th century it was true to say that the more magnificent the individual members' yachts, the finer the club-house.

Two of England's earliest clubs, the Cumberland Fleet, now the Royal Thames Yacht Club, and the Yacht Club, now the Royal Yacht Squadron, started in the tea and coffee houses of London – the Cumberland Fleet in 1775 and the Yacht Club in 1815.

The modern ancestor of the club was brought about by the importation of the coffee bean by the Turkey merchant, David Saunders, who set up his servant, Pasqua Rosee, at Pasqua's Head in St. Michael's Alley, Cornhill, London, in 1652.

Whites Chocolate House was founded in 1698 at the bottom of St. James's Street (now moved appropriately to the top) a year before the Bank of England was founded. The chocolate house initially catered for the public and was open, along with other chocolate and coffee places, to anyone able to lay a penny on the bar on entering. This entitled the subscriber to the use of the room and a news sheet. Gentlemen employed them for most facets of business and pleasure. Those with similar tastes banded together and adopted a particular house.

The History of Whites, published in limited edition by the Hon. Algernon Bourke in 1892, records that:

> 'The special character given to each of the better known houses by its regular customers, did not close it to the general public. Anyone who was decently clad, and could behave himself, was free to enter Whites or any other of the more fashionable houses which were grouped near St. James's Palace. Smoking, we read, was general in all but these few West End houses. Here tobacco was to be found only in the form of finely-scented snuff, "and if any clown, ignorant of the usages of the house, called for a pipe, the sneers of the whole assembly, and the short answers of the waiters, soon convinced him that he had better go somewhere else".'

In this way, White's Chocolate House became adopted by men of fashion and so became known, at least to the rare, as 'the Club'. The proprietor discovered that it was easier and more lucrative to cater for this section of his public and to exclude the others. Other coffee houses had their single interest patrons. Out and out Jacobites, for example, patronised the Cocoa Tree, clergymen went to Childs in St. Paul's Churchyard and for the Cumberland Fleet, Smiths Tea Gardens was the venue. Just before Waterloo, The Yacht Club met at the Thatched House, another coffee house again in St. James's Street, where Swift had also formed a small club called The Brothers.

The formation of The Yacht Club was in part due to the behaviour of Beau Brummel and his 'Dandies'. The Beau had earned the good words of Captain Boteler of the ROYAL SOVEREIGN, as mentioned in Chapter 1, but the behaviour of both his followers and himself at the ballot box at Whites had a hand in persuading Lord Grantham to call a special meeting of that club and to form another of his own, gathering together those gentlemen interested in yachting.

The History of Whites mentions that 'the proceedings at the ballots became almost grotesque. "We must kill that man", a member would say; "it will do him good". "We really cannot have that fellow," said another; "I saw him wearing a white tie in the evening".' Whether these recollections have anything to do with the blackballing of the Foreign Secretary, Lord Castlereagh, three times in 1813, or the exclusion of Mr., later Sir George Wombwell nearly 20 times before he gained entrance, is not recorded.

The Yacht Club, however, came into being as a result of this on June 1st, 1815. It was the first time the word 'club' had been used by 'gentlemen interested in yachting' in mainland Britain. To be elected they had to be 'balloted for at a general meeting consisting of not less than 10 members, the candidates to be proposed and seconded by two members of the Club, two blackballs to exclude.' The original members, of which there were 42, included the Marquess of Thomond, member of the Cork Yacht Club, and the Earl of Uxbridge. Lord Uxbridge was better known as the 1st Marquess of Anglesey and his legendary remark at the Battle of Waterloo and the Duke of Wellington's reply: 'By God', exclaimed Anglesey, 'I've lost my leg', to which the Duke replied, 'Have you by God'. That well known story has a sequel, for his descendant was telling the same story in another London club to an acquaintance. He opened by remarking that his ancestor had lost a leg at Waterloo. To his rage and surprise his companion asked 'which platform'. As he stumped out he met a friend in the corridor and repeated what had just happened, complaining about such a lack of historical grasp. The friend listened and then replied with a laugh, 'as if it mattered which platform'. Such stories are the very stuff of which clubs are made and a good reason to have a meeting place ashore, even if members had their palaces afloat.

It is, therefore, worthwhile looking at the experience of The Yacht Club and the Cumberland Fleet, and in this respect the survey would not be complete without further reference to their organisation and peculiarities wrought by their members.

Although the Cumberland Fleet is an earlier organisation than The Yacht Club, they did not possess a permanent club-house until 1860. By then they were the Royal Thames Yacht Club and had to move from the top of St. James's Street to No. 7 Albemarle Street because of the widening of Piccadilly. Before that the Cumberland Fleet had travelled from their tea rooms to a convenient riverside coffee house at Palace Yard Stairs (Bridge Street) in 1827 and in 1833 to the British Coffee House in Cockspur Street. Their slow progress to a permanent club-house may have been because of the difficulties of obtaining riverside rooms. They had devoted their formative years to organising yacht racing on London's river, then the capital's main thoroughfare. Their efforts were inspired by royalty, for the Duke of Cumberland gave a cup for a race from Westminster Bridge to Putney Bridge and back for pleasure boats of between two and five tons, held on July 11th, 1775.

The Yacht Club's waters, on the other hand, were off Cowes between the Isle of Wight and the mainland. In contrast, their members were not immediately interested in racing, but followed more in the traditions of the Water Club at Cork. The two activities of racing and cruising were apparent at the founding of the two clubs and had developed since Charles II's time. That monarch had been keen on both. Generations of yachtsmen who followed his example in the years to come specialised and produced two distinct breeds – each with their own particular type of yacht. There were those who were interested in cruising and others who were more nakedly competitive and preferred to race. The club-house was found to be a useful aid by the Irish, whose convolutions were more akin to cruising, but that structure was doubly useful to those engaged in racing, for the building not only provided a place to celebrate after a day at sea, but also acted as a race starting and finishing box.

The Yacht Club used the Medina Hotel in East Cowes for meetings and dinners, as many of the original 42 members had been in the habit of spending their summers at Cowes and quite a number rented houses there. The sea port became a watering place of considerable attraction, benefiting from a public mood inspired by George III's passion for the sea at Weymouth and the Prince Regent's exotic attachment to the salt air of Brighton. Bathing in salt-water was considered healthy. Mrs Beeston had set up her salt-water baths at Lymington in the middle of the 18th century. As has been mentioned, people generally preferred to be in the water rather than on it. The Duke of Bedford visited Cowes 'from his rural but delightful cot' at St. Boniface, just north of Ventnor. Again, according to the *Hampshire Courier*, Lord Palmerston took a day trip to Cowes and visited two prison ships before returning to his seat at Broadlands (now the home of Earl Mountbatten of Burma and recently opened to the public). The Duke of Clarence and his sister, Princess Sophia, spent three months there in the late summer of 1811, to the delight of the tradesmen. The Duke liked the place so much he became a member of The Yacht Club in 1817, along with the Prince Regent and the Duke of Gloucester. Lord Grantham had built a little villa just to the west of Cowes Castle for enjoying days on his cutter MERMAID. The *Hampshire Courier* could well report that 'the weather is most delightful and the increase of company adds if possible to the hilarity of this charming spot'.

Regattas had started at Cowes by 1776 as recorded in this painting by Dominic Serres, though the contestants came from the Navy. (Royal Yacht Squadron)

Regattas had already started at Cowes, though the contestants came from the Navy at Portsmouth, as can be seen from the picture by Dominic Serres. This event took place in 1776, a year after the founding of the Cumberland Fleet on the Thames.

The Prince Regent was particularly keen on yachting and The Yacht Club. He gave evidence of his pleasure by conferring the title 'Royal' on the membership in 1820, the first yacht club to gain such a distinction.

Racing was still officially frowned upon. Naval style manoeuvres did not suit everybody though, as a resolution passed on July 29th, 1822 shows:

> 'The original proposition of assembling the vessels of The Club upon certain days under the direction of a leader having been made with a far different view from that of racing and showing superiority of sailing, and inconvenience and danger having arisen from irregularity, it would tend to the comfort of all, and particularly of the ladies who may honour the meeting with their presence, if order were preserved.'

In other words, the yachts were told to keep station. A report from the *Southampton Herald* of August 8th, 1823 shows the sort of thing that went on. Such rigid control was perhaps a little restricting on those with a strong competitive spirit.

> 'The Regatta of last week, having attracted a numerous assemblage of yachts, the sailing meeting took place on the 4th inst. being the first Monday in August, and created considerable observation from its being almost the first time of carrying into effect the new signal code, which was done with much skill and readiness by all the members present. At 10 a.m. the Hon. C.A. Pelham, Commodore for the day, made the signal to sail from the roadstead and on the Squadron being under weigh, to form line on the larboard tack; the Commodore then led to the westward and the yachts worked down as far as Newtown, with a fresh breeze from the southwest. The next signal was to bear up together, and presently afterwards to form in two columns, in which order the squadron led by FALCON, ran for Calshot Castle, and up Southampton Water.
>
> 'At four o'clock the Commodore ordered the fleet to tack, the van division forming ahead, and the rear astern of the FALCON; and having got out of the river, the signal was hoisted to part company, and the several vessels returned to their moorings.'

Sometimes the manoeuvres were more ambitious, therefore more interesting to those who were taking part and hopefully salutory to those watching from the shore, if the *Herald*'s report of August 26th, 1824 is anything to go by:

> 'Nineteen vessels of the Royal Yacht Club, under the direction of Lord Yarborough, the Commodore of the Club, will sail from this port on Monday next for Cherbourg, which will no doubt be a most pleasing, interesting, and novel sight to the French nation, when they behold some of the finest vessels in the world belonging to a club honoured with the patronage of the King, and boasting of the Dukes of Clarence and Gloucester, with a long list of noblemen and most opulent gentlemen in this Kingdom, it presents to the world a phenomenon that none but Englishmen can find pleasure in; but Britain's best bulwarks are her wooden walls, and we are truly gratified in seeing British opulence with so liberal a hand promoting the nursery of our British Tars.'

It was, after all, only nine years since Waterloo, so such a steely-eyed pride was not surprising. Their French hosts obviously did not read the report for they were well received and spent three days in Cherbourg with much ceremony and three in Guernsey before returning to Cowes. Though the 'cruise' was organised as a naval operation, comfort aboard was not forgotten. The reporter from the *Southampton Herald* had a privileged view below and was pleased at what he saw (24.8.24).

'Many of these (Royal Yacht Club) beautiful vessels comprehend all the advantages of the most finished "country villa" besides some which are peculiar to themselves. They have all the accommodation of a house, and are free from the inconvenience of a bad neighbourhood, for their site may be changed at pleasure; they have not only the richest, but also the most varied prospects; they are villas free from house duty and window tax; pay neither tithe nor poor rate; are exempt from government and parochial taxes; and have not only a command of wood and water, but may truly be said to possess the most extensive fishery of any house in England.'

Could there be a more eloquent recital of the advantages of cruising under sail?

Mrs N.M. Condy had a try at both the advantages and disadvantages in her pamphlet 'Reminiscences of a Yachting Cruise' published in 1884. She is writing of August 1843 and a cruise of a squadron of yachts westward from Cowes after the regatta week to Plymouth.

'A week at Cowes is pleasant enough, provided it is the regatta week, and you have a sail every day, and do everything that is to be done in the way of gaiety; so we got on very well, between sails round the island, champagne luncheons, a very pleasant archery meeting at Carisbrooke, and a final wind up with the Royal Yacht Squadron ball, unusually gay and certainly the most amusing one at which I ever had the good fortune to be present.'

Apparently the polka had just arrived.

Mrs Condy and the other guests were taken by gig to the cutter GANYMEDE, or as she refers to it, ANONA, of 69 tons and piped aboard. Two side boys appeared, gangway in hand, and they were supplemented by the bugler who had been asked to play 'Welcome Royal Charlie', but in fact played 'a deadly struggle between "Hearts of Oak" and "The Roast Beef of Old England", the latter decidedly gaining the ascendancy'.

GANYMEDE's owner, whom she described as Mr Matsell, and who was almost certainly J.H.W.P. Smith-Piggott, liked things done naval fashion – 'at times considerably to the discomfort of both himself and his friends'.

Mr Matsell, as we shall call him, followed the signals of the flagship KESTREL, the 202 ton yawl belonging to Lord Yarborough, to the letter.

GANYMEDE had hardly reached Egypt Point when Mr Matsell had to make a signal to the Commodore, for disaster had taken place. The cook had announced 'with a countenance so rueful that, at the very least, I expected the vessel had sprung a leak, was fast filling, and we should soon all be changed into "damp, moist, unpleasant bodies".' The news was almost as serious for the cook had forgotten the laundry. GANYMEDE, therefore requested permission 'to part company'.

In the flukey conditions and with the help of a fair tide, they managed to return to station after picking up the washing. Dinner was served just as the wind freshened and as the yacht heeled, Mrs Condy seized the table, only to be ordered to let go by her host, for it was of the swinging variety. 'I was now compelled to continue my repast in a most decidedly uncomfortable manner, the table being exactly on a level with my nose. The nearest approach to my position, which I can describe, would be sitting on a footstool, hopelessly endeavouring to dine with comfort off the chimney-piece.' The weather deteriorated further and the ladies scrambled into their sanctuary, the ladies cabin.

'By degrees', Mrs Condy remembered, 'I became accustomed to the storm, and not having the least tendency to sea-sickness, was several times on the point of sleep, when my drowsiness was seared away by a most alarming noise, which between the howlings of the storm assumed a most frightful character, sometimes it sounded like a hoarse kind of croaking, then it would change to a long continuous screech, ending in a confused scuffling and gurgling sound which baffled all comparison. At first we thought it must be one of the boys belonging to the yacht, one of whom was a little Frenchman (Antoine) – an odd little creature he was too.' Eventually the ladies could bear it no longer and sought an explanation from the coxswain, Adams. 'Lord love ye, ladies,' exclaimed the sailor, 'it is only the fowls; that bless'd old cock never will let any poor devil sleep after 2 o'clock, and the young'uns are larnin!'

GANYMEDE sought shelter in Weymouth and it being Sunday Mr Matsell determined to achieve an ambition – to hold a church service aboard his yacht in true naval style.

> 'But there was one great difficulty to be surmounted. On board a man-of-war, when divine service is being performed, the church pendant (pennant) is always hoisted at the peak; now a cutter has no peak when the mainsail is furled, so there was nothing for it but to set the mainsail, for I am convinced he would have considered the whole ceremony imperfect had not this important little piece of bunting been displayed to tell heaven what we were about. Accordingly, up went the peak, out flew the flag, and roll, roll went the ANONA, indignantly puzzled to know why her wings were spread after this strange fashion. The captain and crew were summoned; some of them looked cross, others inclined to laugh, but all surprised: for ourselves, we did our best to appear composed and decorous, as we ought to be on such an occasion. But just as the first few prayers were concluded (amongst which Mr Matsell read with most impressive gravity the prayer for all who were at sea, *particularly* the Royal Yacht Squadron), off came a squall from the shore, flap went the mainsail, creak went the boom, down went our little French friend, Antoine, muttering an unholy *sacré*, away went the captain's tarpauling hat, which he had been permitted to retain on the plea of being "roving distracted" with the rheumatics. Whisk it flitted its way through many hands outstretched to save it, and settling on the briny element, walked away astern, as much like a thing of life as those larger floating machines to which it is usual to apply the phrase.
>
> 'A general confusion ensued, Antoine's somersault excited the risible muscles of his juvenile companion, who burst into an uncontrollable fit of laughter; the irate skipper uttered an exclamation totally inconsistent with church pendants; and to crown the whole, the fowls took up the refrain, the cock flapping his wings for a hearty crow, and the hens rushing about the crate adding their cackle to the chorus. Farewell all hopes of a decent conclusion of the service after this, thought I as I glanced at Mr Matsell's face in hopes of meeting something like a smile there to excuse the one that lurked like a truant on my own. Alas! the look of real distress depicted in his disconsolate countenance at the unlucky overthrow of this long-cherished scheme, was quite a reproach to me; but the mixture of contending feelings displayed when he found all his efforts to restore order ineffectual, gave him such a truly ludicrous appearance, that I was obliged to laugh in spite of myself. This put the finishing touch to the matter; and, no longer able to restrain his anger within moderate bounds, he called out furiously, "Boatswain! pipe down and be d—d!" To which the boatswain, who was a bit of a wag, responded a very solemn "Amen!" Thus ended the first and last morning service on board the ANONA.'

While awaiting a fair wind and better weather, they spotted a friend, a Mr Packem, ashore and persuaded him to join the yacht: He was one of those people who make any party go and true to form and to their delight, he plied them with stories. Tucked in the warmth of the saloon, he reminded them of the Irishman at the house of a very hospitable old lady, who was distressed at the delicacy of his appetite.

"'You don't eat Mr O'Brien", she said, pressing some enticing morsel on his plate.

"'No ma'am", he replied, "I don't ate much; but it 'ud do your heart good to see me drink!'"

Whether this story put the following prank into Packem's head Mrs Condy does not tell, but it is certain she must have related her experiences of the night before. At any rate, GANYMEDE was under way and they were round Portland Bill and making across West Bay when the owner was called to look at a crate of fowls by the coxswain.

> '"I say, Adams," again pleaded Mr Matsell, "do come here; don't you think this poor cock's got a cold?"
>
> 'Adams was inexorable; he took another turn before noticing the question in any other way than by a most contemptuous shrug; and when again appealed to, he grumbled out—
>
> '"Devil take the noisy brute; I don't know whether he's got a cold or not, but I wish with all my heart he'd a' got a *sore throat*."
>
> 'Chanticleer's state of health evidently excited no compassion in the unsympathising breast of Mr Adams, and Mr Matsell was lost in conjecture. For my part, I shrewdly suspected Packem had a hand in it; and I shall never forget with what delight he afterwards acknowledged that Adams had told him how we were disturbed by them, and he had stopped the boy who was going to give them their corn, and poured some gin on it, by way of trying a twofold experiment; to see how they would look when they were tipsy; and in hopes of stupifying them sufficiently to keep them quiet till a reasonable hour in the morning. Of course we did not dare breathe it to Mr Matsell, who would never have forgiven him. Nevertheless, I am grieved to say the experiment failed of its desired effect; for the creatures awoke next morning like "giants refreshed," an hour earlier than usual, crowing with renewed vigour.'

GANYMEDE, alias ANONA, reached Torbay and it was 'calm and unruffled as a summer glade'. Lord Yarborough signalled for members to proceed aboard KESTREL, where he extended an invitation for all to dine ashore with him.

The next day the fleet sailed for Plymouth and the Barnpool. As Mrs Condy, Mr Packem and the other guests said their adieux to Mr Matsell, the bugler played 'Should Auld Acquaintance Be Forgot' and in spite of mistakes brought tears to the eyes of the departing, so much so that Packem asked him for 'something jolly'.

'Something jolly was struck up at once; I have no idea what: I never heard any tone resembling it in my life; but most probably it was an impromptu composition.'

There was nothing impromptu about Mrs Condy's opinion of the Commodore: 'None can recall the simple unaffected kindness of his manner to all classes without wishing such a man could live forever'.

The two KESTRELS, a cutter of 156 tons and a yawl of 202 tons, later to be rigged as a brigantine, were his last yachts. The two FALCONS, one a brig and the other ship rigged, preceded the two KESTRELS.

Lord Yarborough's earlier hospitality aboard FALCON at Cowes was legendary. At the close of the 1824 season, as Commodore of the Royal Yacht Club, he invited all those members 'laying in Cowes Roads' and their friends to dine with him aboard his yacht on the Sunday and in spite of the weather being extremely wet, 22 sat down to dinner. On the Monday evening Lord Yarborough organised a ball aboard for 300 guests. He stood at the gangway from 10 to 11 o'clock welcoming the company 'from the numerous assemblage of boats, they did not cease till eleven o'clock. Country dances, quadrilles and Scotch reels, were immediately formed, extending the whole length of the yacht's deck. At two o'clock supper was announced, when the guests descended to the three cabins, the tables of which presented a most sumptuous display of every delicacy that fancy could imagine consisting of jellies, creams, etc.; champagne, Frontignac, and other French wines; and a plentiful supply of fine pines, grapes and other fruit. On withdrawing from the banquet,

The Castle and bathing place at Cowes before the former became the Club-house of the Royal Yacht Squadron. (Cadland Archives)

dancing recommenced and was kept up with greatest spirit and enjoyment till four o'clock, when the boats assembled round the FALCON to convey the visitors to their respective homes; – many of the boats were fitted up as gondolas, with lamps, and had a most pleasing appearance.' (*Southampton Herald*, September 25th, 1824).

According to newspaper reports and at variance with the official history of the Royal Yacht Squadron, the vessel described above was the brig of 150 tons rather than the ship of 351 which was launched at Fishbourne, Isle of Wight on June 6th, 1826, after being christened by Miss Hastings.

Lord Yarborough, who had sat as M.P. for Great Grimsby between 1803 and 1807 and for Lincolnshire between 1807 and 1823, was created Baron Worsley of Appuldercombe after the grandest house on the island, designed in the mood of Vanbrugh (severely damaged by an incendiary bomb in the 1940's, now open to the public). He gave splendid parties there too.

With all this going on a club-house for the R.Y.C. may have seemed unnecessary, but there had to be a focal point. The Medina Hotel at East Cowes served for a time for dinners, meetings and the like, but in 1825 the club held their last meeting for the season in the new club-house on the Parade at West Cowes, which they had taken for a term of years on lease. This was the Gloucester Hotel (now Gloster) named after the Royal Duke. They thought of acquiring more bricks and mortar, too, that year, according to the *Southampton Town & County Herald* which reported 'that the Royal Yacht Club have intentions of purchasing Brownsea Castle (Poole Harbour) as a rendezvous during the summer season'. The idea came to nothing, though just short of 150 years later the John Lewis Partnership followed the thought by taking a lease of the place for the benefit of their staff.

In 1833, during Lord Wilton's Commodoreship, King William IV made it known that 'as a mark of His Majesty's gracious approval of an institution of such national utility, it is His Gracious wish and pleasure that it shall be henceforth known and styled 'The Royal Yacht Squadron' of which His Majesty is graciously pleased to consider himself the head.' More about the 'national utility' later.

Thirty-three years were to go by before the Squadron gave up the lease of the Gloucester and moved to the Castle almost next door. It was an important place, for Cowes derived its name from the two Castles or 'cowes' on either side of the Medina Estuary. The eastern 'cowe' has now disappeared.

The club had outgrown its old premises and there had been a disagreement about the rent. Members decided, therefore, again at the Thatched House in St. James's Street, they accepted an offer of the castle from the Marquess of Conyngham, a past Governor of the Island.

The building was in a terrible state, according to the *Isle of Wight Observer*. 'The celebrated Cowes Castle, once "the lion" of the place, has surrendered itself to the pickaxe of the vandals of the present age'. At any rate, the bill for repairs and new building was estimated at £6,000. This was raised by pledging club savings and issuing bonds to be repaid over a fixed term of years secured against the property.

The result of this effort was not appreciated by the correspondent of *The Observer*, who watched the rebuilding and began his article of May 16th, 1857 with a quotation from Sir Thomas More, Lord Chancellor of Henry VIII who built the original bastion in 1539 and onto which these improvements were secured. Sir Thomas apparently used the sentence frequently: 'To aim at honour here is to set a coat of arms over a prison gate.' The correspondent, obviously pleased with this, developed the theme and went on to say that 'Some have compared the front (of the Castle) to a monastery, and the rear of the building to a nobleman's mews,whilst others have declared it, from its irregular appearance, to resemble a discipline establishment'. He believed that Mr Salvin, the Squadron's architect, could have produced 'a far prettier design at far less cost'.However, he had not yet reached the summit of his disapproval, for he continued 'at the west end, on the site where the famous cookery of the late gallant Marquis stood,has been erected what is termed "the tower" and as such we must call it. One would almost think it had sprung up out of the fumes of the cook's stock pot - a perfect *olla podrida* -a mixture of everything.' The correspondent finished with some good words, though, about the new 'capacious lawn' in place of 'the cankered encumbersome shrubs and overhanging foliage'.

A clue to the writer's tastes is given in his admiration of the Italianate symmetry of the Royal Victoria Yacht Club House at Ryde, designed by Mr W. Huntley of Dover in 1846. In this he was at odds with Sir John Bailey who considered the financial implications of the Squadron's move and who had recommended a levy of £35 per member or an increase in the annual subscription. 'The alternative' Sir John went on to say in his report to the members, 'is fearful to contemplate: inevitable debt, litigation, the loss of our pre-eminence, and the probability of being swallowed up by the Thames, or abdicating in favour of the Victoria'.

The Royal Thames were unaware of all this and were busily recovering from a move of their own to 49 St. James's Street. They were preparing to up sticks yet again to 7 Albemarle Street, because of the widening of Piccadilly.Their Commodore was Lord Alfred Paget, the son of 'One Leg' Anglesey who, as Lord Uxbridge, was a founder member of The Yacht Club. Lord Alfred was Commodore of the Royal Thames from 1846-1873 and with Joseph Weld of Lulworth Castle, a member of the Squadron, did more to advance the sport of sailing than any of his contemporaries.

The Royal Thames continued its London habit but moved from Albemarle Street to 80-81 Piccadilly in 1910 and then in 1922 to a real palace at 60 Knightsbridge.This was one of the finest club-houses in London and suited the change in mood of the club which had originally specialised in the smaller classes of yachts - those under 40 tons - which had been rather forgotten by the Squadron. By 1874 the club fleet in the Nore to Dover race was impressive indeed. Some 17 yachts started, their tonnages varying from 202 tons to 40, and averaging 116. They included the schooner SETONIA owned by Mr W.Turner, the 110 ton yawl CORISANDE, then owned by Mr J.Richardson, of which more later, the famous 117 ton cutter ARROW, the property of Mr Chamberlayne and the schooner GLORIANA of 132 tons, the property of Mr Wilkinson. The club had suffered a little in the 1860's, according to the excellent History of the Cumberland Fleet by Douglas Phillips-Birt, published on the bicentenary of the Royal Thames, by having a club-house in London. Racing between the bridges was no longer practicable, due to the enormous increase in traffic and bridges. The older members were worried that England's most venerable yachting organisation would become 'a mere cheap West End club for gentlemen' and that the sea would be forgotten. Although the club was to go through a few traumas, this worry was never realised and soon after, they moved to their magnificent new club-house.Almeric Paget, created Lord Queenborough, became Commodore. He no doubt chose hit title from Queenborough on the Isle of Sheppey, where Pepys recorded he

Lord Queenborough's achievement with supporters wearing the uniform of the Royal Thames Yacht Club. (Debrett's Peerage Ltd)

put ashore Lady Batten in 1663 because 'she is mighty troublesome on the water'. His heraldic supporters wear the letters R.T.Y.C. on their chests and their boaters.

Up and down the land yachting was being supported by such buildings. The Royal Southern Yacht Club, for example, founded in 1840 at Southampton, had the magnificent Bugle Hall opposite the Royal Pier which, though modified with its Italianate appearance masked, is still particularly pleasant. The later rash of Italianate buildings may have been inspired by the remodelling of Osborne.

Nor should Scotland be forgotten and in this case the size of the yacht was no gauge to the club-house, for the Royal Clyde Yacht Club started off life as the Clyde Model Yacht Club and limited members to yachts of under eight tons. This restraint disappeared after 1863, when 10 and 25 tonners appeared. The photograph shows the original club-house at Hunters Quay before it was destroyed by fire in 1888.

The salt-water palace, however small, required such a gathering place and gentlemen banded together in order to provide this focal point.

The Ballot & Blackball

Not everyone was welcome, though. It was not unreasonable that a bond made by a mutual interest such as sailing, cemented for communal enjoyment, should wish to be selective. Exclusion is as old as the habit of clubbing together. Some people are not clubbable and are too individualistic for the comfort of others. Until recent years, this was felt to be true of the ladies, through the Ladies' Carlton attempted to prove that this was not so. The Royal Yacht Squadron allowed the fair sex to decorate the lawn but denied them the necessary conveniences, for ladies were not allowed inside the Castle. It was the celebrated Rosa Lewis, owner of the Cavendish Hotel, who altered this, but not until 1925. She bought Castle Rock, now the Royal Corinthian Yacht Club, next door, outbidding the Squadron. In 1929 she let her ballroom at the bottom of the garden to the Club, later agreeing to sell it to the Squadron. The ladies, therefore, won their comforts at a stiff price.

Rosa Lewis was very fond of Cowes and 'her little place' there. She was also fond of entertaining those members of the Squadron who had courted her in her youth. Anthony Heckstall-Smith in his classic 'Sacred Cowes' quoted her as remarking caustically, but no doubt with a twinkle, 'While they won't 'ave me on their old lawn, I 'ave to let their lady friends into my garden to piddle'.

Gentlemen suffered a more dramatic form of exclusion – by the little cork blackball. The same that the 'Dandies' had rolled so irreverently in the elections at Whites Club and so led to the conception of the Squadron, as mentioned earlier. Blackballing was slow to start in The Yacht Club, but in due course, was turned into an art by a few. J.B.G. in *The Sporting Magazine* remembers little of this activity before King William IV's reign. There was the Duke of Buckingham who was not re-elected after failing to pay his subscription. The other case was rather more celebrated for he was 'the owner of a yacht like a river barge with a flat bottom, and he was excluded more in joke than otherwise, it being reputed that she was two months in her voyage from the Thames to Cowes, and that moreover the bulkhead and chimney in the cabin were of brick.'

Such an aversion to smoke led to the banning of steam power in The Yacht Club vessels. No member owning such a beast could be considered for election and anyone

Bugle Hall, Southampton, the headquarters of the Royal Southern Yacht Club. (British Yachts and Yachtsmen)

The Royal Clyde Yacht Club at Hunters Quay before the building was destroyed by fire in 1888. (British Yachts and Yachtsmen)

already owning one had to resign. The *Southampton Herald* in 1825 led the way with the complaint that smoke from steamers obscured the opposite shore of the Solent so that the New Forest and Calshot Castle were all but blotted out and 'the murky vomitings of the furnaces covered the Southampton Water from side to side'. The rule was succinct and exclusion was as sure as the blackball:

'Resolved that as a material object of this Club is to promote seamanship and the improvement of sailing vessels, to which the application of steam engines is inimical, no vessel propelled by steam shall be admitted into the Club and any members applying a steam engine to his yacht shall be disqualified thereby and cease to be a member'. One of the casualties of this rule was Thomas Assheton-Smith, a yachtsman in the model of Lord Alfred Paget and Joseph Weld. As the rule was passed he was building the 400 ton, 120′ steam yeacht MENAI.

Assheton-Smith was a pioneer and not to be hampered by such social distinctions. He had built five sailing yachts before his passion for experiment had led him to steam. Seven steam-powered vessels followed, all with evocative names. He built FIRE KING in 1840, succeeded by three FIRE QUEENs, a JENNY LIND and a SEA SERPENT.

The very convenience of steam wore down members' objections, for by 1843 they were weakening to the point of a joke by passing a resolution 'that steamers belonging to the Squadron shall consume their own smoke'. A year later, steamers of over 100 hp qualified for admission and the privileges of the Squadron. In 1853 all reference to disqualification for using artificial power in yachts was deleted. That did not end the unpopularity of the steamer though among a substantial proportion of yachtsmen and Sir Edward Sullivan voiced that opinion when writing the Introduction to the Badminton Library's 'Yachting', first published in 1885. He felt that the repeal of the Royal Yacht Club 1827 rule against members owning steam yachts was ill conceived. The idea was based on a widely held view at the time – that steam destroyed seamanship. Sir Edward Sullivan's Introduction to that early comprehensive treatise 'Yachting', which was part of the Sports and Pastimes series, was in no doubt, for he wrote:

'Steam does destroy seamanship; a steamship hand is certainly not half a sailor. Now more than half the tonnage of the Club is in steamers. I think it is a pity, and they are such steamers

"SUNBEAM"

52

too! 800 tons, 1,000 tons, 1,500 tons. I do not see where they are to stop; but, I believe that in this, as in most things, we have run into excess. I cannot believe that the largest steam yacht afloat, with all the luxury and cost that upholsterers and cabinet-makers can devise, will ever give a man who is fond of the sea and seafaring matters a tithe of the gratification that a 100-ton sailing vessel will afford; one is a floating hotel, the other is a floating cottage. I prefer the cottage.'

Lord Cardigan, later hero of the Crimea, was not universally popular among yachtsmen. He was blackballed for this reason rather than the fact that he owned a schooner with auxiliary steam power. He enjoyed the comfort of yachting and used ENCHANTRESS as a bivouac at the Crimea rather than roughing it with his men. Once while sailing, he was asked by his skipper 'Will you take the helm my Lord?' To which he replied, 'No thank you, I never take anything between meals'.

ENCHANTRESS was owned later, in 1868, by Sir Percy Shelley. In the 60's of the last century, Sir Percy was suspected by the 'Pirate', the owner of a 150 ton black hulled, 16 gun schooner, of being responsible for his rejection in a Squadron ballot. The 'Pirate' decided to obtain appropriate satisfaction and anchored his vessel off the Castle and ran out the highly polished guns on the landward side. He sent his boat ashore with a note for the 4th Baronet, demanding an apology and threatening to open fire if this was not forthcoming within half an hour.

Sir Percy was dining in the Castle at the time with Sir Allen Young. He was incensed and refused to do any such thing. Sir Allen, however, realising that the 'Pirate' was capable of anything, reminded Sir Percy of the inconvenience of being bombarded during dinner. Sir Percy saw the force of this and sent the required note, on receipt of which the 'Pirate' dipped his ensign and sailed away. The story was told by Sir Allen Young, who owned ten yachts during his 29 year membership of the Squadron. This was the same number of vessels accumulated over 46 years by his dinner companion of that night. The scene of the two in the Castle and the 'Pirate' anchored off the battery, produces a vivid picture that can still be imagined in that unchanging place today.

Much later, Sir Henry Dennison, was alleged to say that he always blackballed people when the wind was in the east. The author can remember Ronald Sloane Stanley warning a younger man of over 50, who, he said, had suggested that less ripe members be put forward for election. 'Young man', he warned, 'remember that this is an old man's club'.

Other clubs had their 'assassins' too who no doubt reacted to other wind directions. Candidates were 'pilled' for lesser reasons than the weather. One gentleman, for example, always kept out those whose names began with the same letter, so that he could continue his exclusive use of that compartment in the club's letter rack.

The National Utility

Social antics at the ballot box and festivities afloat and ashore, tended to draw attention from the real contribution that yachtsmen were making to naval architecture. The efficient use of the wind, and later power, were as much goals for the Navy as they were for yachtsmen.

The Royal Yacht Club, for example, had included several who were particularly interested in the science of shipbuilding, though not necessarily motivated towards

Lord Brassey's SUNBEAM, *one of the first round-the-world yachts.*
(Beken of Cowes)

53

producing a fast racing yacht. Lord Yarborough, Commodore of the Royal Yacht Club, whose entertainments aboard his FALCON have already been described, was one of these. He demonstrated in the 1820's, the superior design of his vessel to Sir Edward Codrington, by joining the Admiral's fleet in the Channel while they were cruising. His sailors were a match for the Royal Navy too for they had voluntarily consented to the use of the cat-o'-nine tails as a punishment, each signing a paper setting forth 'the usefulness of a sound flogging in cases of extremity'.

Revenue cutters, considered the fastest of the government vessels, were beaten by yachts until the service recognised the value of such amateur experience and commissioned the famous Cowes yacht builder, Joseph White, to build the revenue cutter VIGILANT, which beat Lord Anglesey's PEARL and Lord Belfast's HARRIET. Such was the interest in these developments that John Fincham, the Superintendent of Naval Architecture at Portsmouth had a close look at the five famous Royal Yacht Club vessels in 1827. They were the second FALCON, COQUETTE, PEARL, NAUTILUS and DOLPHIN.

Fincham observed that the yachtsmen's advantage in experiment came as a direct result of a single-minded interest. He observed that, 'most improvements have their origin in individual exertions, but the extent and rapidity of their advancement are generally proportionate to the importance attached to them and the support they receive from men of influence and fortune, who may be interested in their promotion. The advantages derived from The Yacht Club are in this respect very great'.

The Squadron, under its guise as the Royal Yacht Club and in its later history, was much aided in this advance by admitting to the membership many distinguished naval officers. Among these was Captain J.C. Symonds, R.N., owner of the yawl ADMIRAL CORNWALLIS, who later became Surveyor to the Navy, who owed a great deal to his work with yachts of the Club. He designed the Pantomine class, four vessels taking their names from that type of play. COLUMBINE was designed for the Navy, HARLEQUIN for Lord Vernon, and she proved faster than Lord Yarborough's FALCON, CLOWN for the Duke of Portland and finally PANTALOON, again for the Duke of Portland and the most successful of the four, which was later bought by the Royal Navy.

The design for PANTALOON had been properly thought out, as might be expected of the Duke, a man of some genius, who had built Troon Harbour and was descended from the 4th Duke, who gave Stephenson his first order for a locomotive. Designer Symonds was sent for and went to Welbeck Abbey and then on to Fullerton House, Ayrshire. There, with Thompson, the Duke's master shipwright, they conducted one of the first 'tank tests', for five small replicas of about 10 tons, with such names as PUNCHINELLO and GRIMALDI, which had been previously prepared with different proportions of length, beam and draught. A similar scale model of the Navy's 10 gun brig had also been constructed as a comparison. In these 'tests', the model of PANTALOON was decidedly superior and so she was decided upon.

This flowering of genius did not impress the highly competitive Lord Belfast, who commissioned Joseph White of Cowes, in 1832, to build him WATERWITCH. Lord Belfast's aggressive spirit was to cost him friends in the end. He was Commodore of the Squadron for only a year before being voted out of office.

Lord Belfast selected the 10 gun brig for his improvements, hardly a propitious choice, for this class of warship had a poor reputation in the Navy and was known variously as 'things' or 'coffin brigs'. They were poor sailors and so usually over-canvassed to extract

Two views of the America's Cup Challenger
GALATEA – *above and below deck.*
(Beken of Cowes)

the last ounce of speed. This often proved too much and many were lost. Belfast specified that WATERWITCH should be fitted out to naval standards with guns of the same size and weight. For trials he took her to join in exercises with the Royal Navy off Cork and she performed magnificently. WATERWITCH out sailed and out pointed the Navy's crack ships. The people of Cowes were delighted when they heard the news, but her success was a rod to the Navy's back. Captain Symonds was criticised, though he had produced the successful predecessors that had sparked WATERWITCH. Symonds was not, however, without his supporters. WATERWITCH, in the meantime, used to lie off Portsmouth waiting for one of the Surveyors to the Navy's ships, then proceeded to out sail her. On one celebrated occasion, Lord Belfast reduced sail pointedly to keep station when accompanying Her Majesty's Ship VESTAL with Princess Victoria and her mother aboard.

In 1834, two years after WATERWITCH's launch, just after Lord Belfast had reduced her to a yacht and fitted her out to a high standard of comfort, the Navy bought her. Joseph White had produced a vessel with a finer entry and sweeter lines than the bluff bows, round midship section and finer stern of her predecessors. This traditional look was known as 'cod's head and mackerel tail'.

The efforts of Lord Yarborough, The Duke of Portland, Lord Vernon, Lord Belfast and Captain Symonds and the support of the Isle of Wight builders like List of Fishbourne, who built the Pantomine class and White of Cowes, led to William IV's wish that such 'national utility' should be rewarded and the Royal Yacht Club became the Royal Yacht Squadron for this signal service.

The progress in design also contributed to the weatherliness of the large auxiliary

Lieutenant William Henn, Royal Navy (Rtd) with his whale's tooth walking stick. (British Yachts and Yachtsmen)

Part of the after guard of the America's Cup Challenger GALATEA. The monkey, Peggy, was active aboard helping in hoisting and lowering sail. When GALATEA was ahead in a race, she would run out to the bowsprit end and jump up and down as if to urge the vessel on. The skipper of GALATEA thought that Peggy gave lie to Darwin's theory that man was descended from monkeys. He believed that Peggy had descended from man a few pegs and had then 'hove to'. (Ian Dear)

cruising yacht and was a significant step in the creation of the large sailing yachts of the latter half of the century that made comfortable world cruising in vessels such as SUNBEAM and VALHALLA not only possible, but successful.

The Squadron and the Royal Thames, particularly the latter, were struggling with the problem of how best to match yachts of unequal size in competition. The measurement of size had been achieved by the tonnage laws enacted by Parliament in 1694 and this employed a length of keel measurement. Using this measurement, the longer the keel the greater was the tonnage. The speed of the vessel, though, depended more on the length of water-line and so if the bow and stern were heavily raked, the keel measurement dropped without materially altering the speed. This, of course, was the important measurement and, therefore, it was possible to cheat the rule. To prevent this, it was proposed to take the measurement between the stem and the sternpost at deck level. The Royal Thames Yacht Club, however, came up with the best idea of all and this was 'Thames tonnage measurement' or tons T.M. Described mathematically, it looked like this:

$$\frac{(\text{Length} - \text{Beam}) \times \text{Beam} \times \frac{1}{2} \text{Beam}}{94} = \text{Tons T.M.}$$

Viewed another way, the need for such a rule marked the beginning of an expensive slide into racing by numbers, where performance had more to do with the slide rule than the helmsman's clever touch on the tiller. This process was to reach absurd proportions in later years, for the racing boat became markedly less seaworthy and pinched below, to the point of discomfort, separating still further the cruising yachtsman and seaman from the racing man who was, and perhaps still is, prepared to throw away sound seamanship practice and the delights of 'a home at sea' in pursuit of speed round the buoys. The requirements of the New York Yacht Club for the America's Cup, of which more later, muted the effects of the out and out racing rules by requiring the challenger, at least until the last war, to sail across the Atlantic for the Race. Such a requirement made her less of a racing machine. However, in 1886 when GALATEA challenged, the owner's requirements made matters very different. GALATEA was owned by Lt. Henn, who had resigned his commission in the Navy so that he could devote all his energies to sailing. GALATEA was his home and he lived aboard with his wife and every comfort. On deck, everything was there that could be expected of a challenger for the America's Cup in the late 80's of the last century. Below, however, it was laid out like a Victorian house, the saloon more like a drawing room.

The extra weight of all this finery may have been partially responsible for his defeat by the defender MAYFLOWER. GALATEA was certainly outclassed by the American yacht, designed by Edward Burgess and skippered by the famous 'Hank' Haff, for MAYFLOWER won the first match by 12 mins. 1 second on corrected time and the final match by 29 mins. 9 seconds, again corrected time.

William Henn was an Irishman, born in County Clare, and he and his wife were used to living afloat. In the 80 ton yawl GERTRUDE, they had sailed some 49,000 miles in seven years. He had joined the Royal Navy in 1860 and was aboard the crack frigate GALATEA as a midshipman, before being selected to command the Royal Society's expedition in search of Livingstone. Henn began his yachting in an open lugger-rigged whale boat, in which he cruised round Ireland.

Mrs Henn had GALATEA built and chose Beavor-Webb as the designer. The original challenge was a joint one with Sir Richard Sutton's GENESTA, but something went wrong

Over 500 tons.

s. Victoria & Albert	5005
s. Standart	4334
s. Hohenzollern	3773
s. Mahroussa	3581
s. Poliarnaia Zvezda	3270
s. Valiant	2184
s. Alexandra	2157
s. Maha Chakri	2092
s. Lysistrata	2089
s. Iolanda	1822
s. Nahma	1806
s. Semiramis	1797
s. Hirondelle	1771
s. Atmah	1746
s. Giralda	1664
s. Glencairn	1571
s. Aphrodite	1529
s. Valhalla	1490
s. Niagara	1441
s. Sapphire	1421
s. Triad	1413
s. Atalanta	1398
s. Corsair	1396
m. Y. Ddraig Goch	1390
s. Princesse Alice	1368
s. Albion	1346
s. Alberta	1322
s. Cassandra	1280
s. Warrior	1266
s. Erin	1242

(s. – steam yacht,
m. – yacht fitted with motor)

Yachts over 500 tons from Lloyd's Register of Yachts for 1913.

with the ballasting. GENESTA went alone but failed against PURITAN in 1885, leaving GALATEA to come over the following year, with Mrs Henn aboard, confirming her record as the first lady to cross the Atlantic in a racing yacht.

The 90 ton racing cutter GALATEA was 102′ 7″ overall, 87′ on the water-line and had a beam of 15′ and a draught of 14′. She carried 8,230 square feet of sail, no mean feat on a cutter, when compared with today's three masted topsail schooner SIR WINSTON CHURCHILL of 135′ overall, carrying 7,110 square feet.

GALATEA's Thames tonnage would have been 104, while SIR WINSTON CHURCHILL is 297. GALATEA, of course, was canvassed as an out and out racing yacht, for all her pretentions below, while the 81-year younger SIR WINSTON CHURCHILL is a training vessel, requiring a less demanding spread of sail.

Thames tonnage is used by Lloyd's Register of Yachts and is still the way of measuring the size of a yacht, though it was not used for rating and handicapping after 1882, when the Yacht Racing Association system was introduced. A glance at the league table for 1913, according to this measurement of tonnage, shows just how magnificent these figures can be.

The Ensign

The 'national utility' of the Royal Yacht Squadron was recognised as early as 1829, for the Admiralty issued warrants enabling members to wear the White Ensign of the Royal Navy from that date. The Club changed their burgee to a red cross with crown in the centre on a white ground to compliment that beautiful flag. This Club was not alone, though, in enjoying the privilege, for the Royal Thames and the Royal Western, among others, held a warrant for flying the white. The Royal Cork, on the other hand, wore the red.

The advantage enjoyed by the Royal Yacht Squadron was that their members' vessels were classed as warships, exempting them from harbour dues. It was for the convenience of foreign harbour masters that they were given the privilege of the Royal Navy's flag.

The plain white flag with the jack in the corner, though, was worn by other clubs, including the Royal Western. Their Irish members formed their own Club, the Royal Western Yacht Club of Ireland, and they pleaded with the Admiralty for a real privilege – to wear a green ensign. The Admiralty refused, not out of any colour sense, but because they could not sanction another colour to be worn by British ships. The Irish, no doubt disappointed, then plumped for the white, with a crown and a pale wreath of shamrocks near the fly to add that subtle touch of green.

The advantages enjoyed by the Squadron became attached to the flag, and were therefore accorded to other clubs, no doubt again 'for the convenience of the foreign harbour masters'. With the white flag, with or without the red cross, flying from so many staffs in harbour and 'after peaks' at sea, it was inevitable that some would abuse the Navy's flag and the privileges granted to it. The 'Memorials of the Royal Yacht Squadron' record 'there was a continual correspondence between the Admiralty and the Secretary of the Squadron on the subject during those years (1829-1842) which is preserved at the Castle and goes to show that a great part of that gentleman's time was spent in explaining that such and such a vessel which had committed such and such an outrage, at Lisbon or Marseilles or Naples, had no connection with the Club'. The situation became so bad that

ROYAL YACHT SQUADRON.   RUSSIAN.

A certificate of membership of the Royal Yacht Squadron for the benefit of foreign harbour masters. It was available in many languages. (Royal Yacht Squadron)

ROYAL YACHT SQUADRON

The undersigned secretary of the Yacht Club hereby certifies that the pleasure yacht (yacht de plaisance), called _____ and registered under no. ____ at the port of _____ with a tonnage of _____, the owner of which is _____, is the same as that entered on the record signed by me and addressed to the General Directorate of Customs in Russia, and that the said _____ is a member of the Yacht Club and that the said yacht does not perform any commercial operations.

In respect whereof I request from the Russian Government the privilege of exemption from shipping duties. In addition, the above vessel conforms to the regulations laid down.

Cowes, dated: _____

Secretary

Lord Yarborough asked the Admiralty for permission to wear the blue instead of the white, to stop this 'undeserved disgrace'. The Admiralty, however, would not allow this and in 1842 gave the Squadron the sole use of the white ensign – or so they thought – for they failed to notify the Irish section of the Royal Western, relying on their English parent. The Squadron became the unique holder when the Admiralty, rather belatedly, for it was 12 years later, discovered their error.

The Squadron used to help members 'remind foreign harbour masters' of their Royal Naval status by supplying an impressive printed form.

Before leaving the Club ashore, a word about dress. The Royal Yacht Club adopted a recognised uniform in 1826 – 'a common blue jacket with white trousers'. It was in the style of a pea jacket, commonly referred to as a bum freezer. The minutes are apt, for they continue, 'and to such as are not too square in the stern it is far from being an unbecoming dress'. There were, however, the comment continued, 'some strange figures of gentlemen sailors at the Cowes Regatta, and they ought to have their pictures taken'.

The dress for the ball in 1882 was a short, round jacket with brass buttons. These were later replaced with black, engraved with the monogram in gold. It was reasoned that brass buttons were reserved for the crew. Other clubs followed in adopting nautical wear for the evening. Most of them did not have the same reservations about brass.

Whether appearance from aft or 'cool winds under the counter' inspired change in the day rig is not known, but the pea jacket gave way to the single-breasted jacket such as Lt. Henn is wearing, or the double-breasted watch coat, with or without waistcoat.

Clothes generally had a heavy look about them, as if summer weather was something that either seldom happened, or should be ignored. By the end of the century the yachting cap was worn by everyone. It took different forms, usually variations of the naval cap with a small cloth covered peak and narrow crown. Yacht clubs generally adopted a distinctive badge of their own design to decorate the silk woven band.

By the 80's, the ladies looked as elegant afloat as they did ashore, but Cowes itself had altered. The quiet, family watering place and port had changed since the early days of The Yacht Club. The attentions of royalty, in particular the Prince of Wales, the love of the Queen for her house at Osborne and for her yacht VICTORIA & ALBERT II, had acted as a prime example to others, who came to see what was going on. The 'Memorials' quote comment of the day:

> 'It is no longer a small family party who come down to live seafaringly with their lovers and brethren, but a large crowd, mostly of new people, who flit in and out of the little town with one object of showing dresses, seeing the last new beauties, and keeping clear of the hated sea.'

The Squadron steps themselves were said to have been built as an aid to ladies. A contemporary account is even more particular, for – 'A few years ago it was pointed out that the R.Y.S. landing was desperately inconvenient to *ladies' maids*. At low water it was not nearly so easy to come alongside as it was to draw up at the door of Mr Peter Robinson's shop in Oxford Street in a brougham and there were some nasty rocks near it which were much in the way'. The new landing did not seem to have the Oxford Street touch though, 'for a boat from Lord Bute's yacht with ladies aboard was stove in and sunk, Lady Howard of Glossop being thrown into the water in circumstances of some danger', according to the Memorials. Lord Bute, the 3rd Marquess, owned the 260 ton schooner LADY-BIRD for some 20 years, between 1867 and 1887, and the unfortunate Lady Howard was his mother-in-law.

Some members of the Royal Yacht Squadron around the turn of the century. (Royal Yacht Squadron)

1. Duke of Rutland.
2. Viscount Bangor.
3. Lord Otho FitzGerald, M.P.
4. Charles Birch, Esq.
5. Sir Reginald Graham, Bart.
6. John Doherty, Esq.
7. Earl of Hardwicke.
8. C. J. Lambert, Esq.
9. E. A. Drummond, Esq.
10. C. Milward, Esq., Q.C.
11. Count Batthyany.
12. Lord Dorchester.
13. Duke of Marlborough, K.G.
14. H. Pakenham-Mahon, Esq.
15. Lord Rendlesham.
16. Lieut R. C. Tyllier Blunt, R.N.
17. Commander R. C. Tatnall, R.N.

18. Montague J. Guest, Esq.
19. F. A. Hankey, Esq.
20. Hugh C. Trevanion, Esq.
21. A. J. Scott, Esq.
22. J. Mulholland, Esq.
23. Sir R. Sutton, Bart.
24. Tyrwhitt Walker, Esq.
25. Marquis of Drogheda.
26. Lt.-Col. J. B. Sterling.
27. Lindesay Shedden, Esq.
28. F. C. Ashworth, Esq.
29. Rt. Hon. T. Milner-Gibson.
30. Marquis of Ailsa.
31. Colonel Charles Baring.
32. Marquis of Londonderry, K.P.,
    (Vice-Commodore).
33. Earl of Wilton, G.C.H.,
    (Commodore).

34. H.R.H. The Prince of Wales, K.G.
35. Lord Hastings.
36. Sir Allen Young.
37. C. Davies Gilbert, Esq.
38. Vice-Admiral, The Hon. G. D. Keane,
    (Hon. Member).
39. Richard Grant, Esq.,
    (Secretary).
40. E. N. Harvey, Esq.
41. Lt.-Col. Henry Armytage.
42. Adrian Hope, Esq.
43. Earl of Wicklow.
44. Captain E. R. Boyle.
45. C. A. W. Rycroft, Esq.
46. R. W. Spicer, Esq.
47. A. Congreve, Esq.

48. Sir Thomas Erskine, Bart.
49. Sir J. M. Burgoyne, Bart.
50. Earl of Gosford, K.P.
51. Sir Thomas Whichcote, Bart.
52. Inglis Jones, Esq.
53. Earl De-la-Warr and Buckhurst.
54. Revd. J. N. Palmer.
55. J. Wardlaw, Esq.
56. John Blackett, Esq.
57. John Tremayne, Esq.
58. Sir G. Stucley, Bart.
59. T. Greg, Esq.
60. R. B. Sheridan, Esq.
61. Colonel J. Campbell.
62. P. Perceval, Esq.
63. Waiter (William).

Top left
Lord Fitzwilliam, Lady Fitzwilliam, Hon. F. Dawnay aboard Lord Fitzwilliam's KATHLEEN R.Y.S. (Cadland Archives)

Top right
An unknown group about to go ashore, at Cowes. (David Couling)

Above left
Yachting with a capital 'Y'. A sailing party aboard SKJAGGEDAB FROS *in 1879* (Radio Times Hulton Picture Library)

Above right
Mrs. Godfrey Baring, Lord Hyde, Mrs Rupert Beckett, Mr E. Fitzgerald with Captain Pooley aft of the Mizzen, aboard BRUNETTE R.Y.S. (Cadland Archives)

A glance at family photographs at sea in the last thirty years of the 19th century and the early part of the 20th gives a feeling of tranquillity. Part of the reason was, of course, the requirements of the camera itself. It was difficult to take action shots with such slow film or subject the mechanism to the rigours of the weather at sea. This was not the principal reason though, for neither of the sexes, particularly the ladies, made any concession to sport. They dressed to complement their friends, to decorate the group, whether ashore or afloat.

Sartorial Elegance Afloat
(Royal Yacht Squadron)

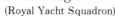

The Earl of Dunraven

The Earl of Lonsdale (The Yellow Earl)

General Sartorius VC

Frederick Dugmore

Philip Percival

Bertie Mitford

61

CHAPTER III

The Salt-Water Palace and the Fashionables

The tranquil period of the last quarter of the 19th century, together with the thirst for speed and comfort at sea, enabled the yacht to develop. The large cruising yacht and the racing vessel blossomed side by side and both could be seen in Cowes Roads, bracing themselves for high entertainment and keen competition. Steam was playing an increasing part in this flowering.

Dixon Kemp, in his two volume survey 'Yacht and Boat Sailing' sums up the choice open to those able to contemplate the larger vessel at that time. He recommends, with his usual common sense, 'that in selecting a yacht, a man, as in making other purchases, will be guided by his tastes and by his means'. The beginner, fired with enthusiasm for the sea, he advises, should start off small and grow bigger and so learn the rudiments of seamanship and yacht management the hard way. In this early period he should have nothing larger than he can skipper himself. However, in tune with the age, his recommendation was for a much larger vessel than would be the case today, for he believed the young sailor should begin his apprenticeship aboard a five, 10 or 20 rater. Dixon Kemp was using the newfangled Y.R.A. rating system, which was adopted in preference to Thames tonnage for the purposes of promoting competition in 1887. The mathematics of the rule looked like this:

$$\frac{\text{Sail Area} \times \text{Loaded Waterline Length}}{6000} = \text{Rating}$$

In modern terms this meant that he was recommending that a beginner's yacht should be between the extremes of a 24 footer with the unbelievable sail area of 1,250 square feet to a 50 footer with 2,500 square feet of canvas.

Dixon Kemp recognised, though, that there were some who could well prefer to jump such uncomfortable acquaintance with the water. He recognised that 'living in a 10 rater, or 40 footer, to many young yachtsmen might be utter misery, and perhaps death. The budding yachtsman who has been in the habit, perhaps, of spending a couple of hours every morning over his toilet, surrounded by all the luxuries of the upholsterer's art – velvet pile carpet, satin cretonne, cheval glasses, water colour drawings, Dresden china – and perhaps a *valet de chambre*. The man who has been used to such luxuries as these must have a big schooner or yawl.'

Dixon Kemp realised that there were those who just had to have the best, even if they had had little to do with the sea before. 'If the dawning yachtsman', he continues, 'has boundless wealth, is a little of a sybarite, and determines to spend two or three months afloat because it is the fashion, he, too will get a yacht to his taste; but she will probably be a large steamer, unless he has determined on racing, when a large schooner, yawl or cutter would be chosen.'

The purpose of this chapter is to look at the yachts that might be chosen by the sybarite and by those Dixon Kemp would have said possessed 'boundless wealth'. However, a few of them may nevertheless have adopted his maxim of graduating from the smaller classes first. They would have spent their apprenticeship with the wind on the cheek, watching the sea race along the deck, before taking a well-deserved rest in the cane chair, under the

Opposite
VALHALLA R.Y.S.was constructed for Joseph Laycock in 1892. Bought by Lord Crawford in 1902, she was one of the few fully rigged yachts and the best example of a steam auxiliary ever built. (Beken of Cowes)

*Quiet moments on deck –
The sun and the smell of warm teak. Lord
Cecil Manners and Lady Fitzwilliam
aboard* KATHLEEN R.Y.S.
(Cadland Archives)

It was possible for guests to achieve this aboard both the cruising and the racing yacht, even when the latter was pursuing her purpose. Many of the large schooners, ketches and yawls managed to race and to cruise. A prime example of this ambivalence was CARIAD I.

Her success as both a racing and a cruising yacht, gave her a long life, as such dexterity, born of good design, often achieved in other yachts and working vessels. An example of this today is the London Sailing Project's ketch RONA, built by Stow & Sons of Shoreham in 1895 and still taking young people to sea after 84 years. There is no better example, though, than the remarkable survival of BOADICEA, a Maldon oyster smack, built in 1808 and still fishing, 171 years later.

CARIAD I was built a year after RONA, in 1896, by Summers & Payne of Southampton to the designs of A.E. Payne for Lord Dunraven. She was 129 tons T.M., 88'.6" overall, 18'.6" beam with a draught of 10.85 feet. CARIAD was of composite construction, wood planking on steel frames.

Lord Dunraven took CARIAD to Lisbon in 1898 as part of the tercentenary celebrations of the doubling of the Cape of Good Hope by Vasco da Gama, for he was the delegate from the Royal Geographical Society. Part of the celebration was a yacht race and this CARIAD won handsomely. Lord Dunraven, however, thought his finest triumph in Portugal was a speech he made after the race in praise of Henry the Navigator, Vasco da Gama and the Portuguese nation generally. He said afterward that it was 'the most comfortable speech I ever made, for I spoke in English in the happy assurance that nobody understood what I was saying'.

Lord Dunraven sold CARIAD I at the turn of the century to J.B. Millar, as a new CARIAD lee of the deckhouse, with the cap pulled down over the eyes listening to sea sounds and experiencing the sweet smell of sun-warmed varnish or scrubbed teak.

CARIAD I built for Lord Dunraven, owned in this picture by J.B. Millar. Her steam launch is on the davits. (John Millar)

was being designed by A.E. Payne. CARIAD II was 6′ longer, with a foot more beam, but the same draught. This put the Thames measurement up by 33 tons. The new yacht was a great racing success, winning the R.Y.S. King's Cup three times, so that it now has pride of place in the hall of the family seat at Adare Manor.

J.B. Millar used CARIAD I as a cruising yacht and she carried a steam launch on davits. In this he followed the advice of Napoleon I's brother, Prince Jerome. Like his nephew Napoleon III, the Prince was interested in yachting and he is credited with bringing to the notice of English yachtsmen the convenience of a steam tender. The 'Memorials' record how 'social Cowes, after 1881, went to luncheon, to dinner, to church, and paid calls, on board steam launches'. The Millar family were keen on steam, too, as will be discovered. J.B. Millar sold CARIAD and she is still in existence, now chartering in the Caribbean.

Before considering the out and out racing yacht whose only cruises were between different starting lines, it is worth looking at the large cruising yacht more closely to see how far comfort and sea keeping had become happily entangled.

The Cruising Yacht

The large cruising yacht could be divided into three main classes: The pure sailing yacht without steam or later motor – these were often raced, sometimes extensively, and particularly successfully as exampled by CARIAD. Other owners occasionally dabbled in the sport to give a little further amusement. These were in the cruiser racer tradition started by Charles II. The next class was the fully rigged steam or auxiliary that also competed, but rather less often, and were developed for extensive cruising. Lastly, there was the fully powered steam yacht, with or without auxiliary sails, that only raced through exuberance.

Perhaps the first matter that owners of the first of these classes, the large sailing yacht, had to think about after a peep in his pocket, was the rig. Should she be a cutter, a yawl, a ketch or a schooner?

Such consideration is, of course, valuable to the man about to devote his time to racing, as it is to the cruising yachtsman who regards rapid footfalls on the deck and the scream of blocks tortured to gain seconds, as an anathema. Both, to a degree, would like to obtain the best out of their yachts. Consider then the alternatives. The yawl gained over the cutter through lighter spars and rigging and on a 90 ton vessel the difference would be nearly 2,000 pounds. To the technically minded, this would be the equivalent of moving two tons of top tier inside ballast and adding it to the outside keel. More visible, however, would be the savings that could be achieved in turning a cutter into a yawl, in reducing the length of bowsprit and boom. Cutters of those days had magnificent spars over the bows and hanging over the stern. For example, the then yawl rigged CORISANDE of 153 tons had a bowsprit outboard of 35′ on her overall length, excluding this spar, of 93′. Her gaff and boom were 42′ and 61′ 6″ respectively on her last alteration. OIMARA, one of the noblest of all fore and aft vessels, built in 1867 by Messrs. Robert Steele & Co. of Greenock for Charles Tennant, had magnificent dimensions. This 165 ton cutter was 97′ overall, excluding spars, and had a bowsprit of 47′ outboard with a boom of 70′ and a gaff of 47′. She carried 5,500 square feet of sail. Today a Class I ocean racer, such as Ted Heath's MORNING CLOUD, has no bowsprit, a mast height above the deck of nearly 57′ and a boom length of 14′.

These dimensions show the difference between the cutter and the yawl of a similar size. Conversion to this two masted rig could, therefore, save 20% in the outboard length of spars. FLORINDA, 138 tons, was converted from a cutter to a yawl and in this, 15′ was lopped off the boom and her bowsprit came down 20% to 36′.

The problem with the yawl was, and perhaps still is, that a vessel so rigged does not go to windward as well as a cutter. Dixon Kemp was categorical about the designs of his day. 'A cutter, with a true wind', he stated, 'will beat as far to windward in a day, as a yawl will in a day and a quarter; will walk off with a light air when the yawl will scarcely move; and in a breeze under topsail is even more comfortable and easy than a yawl. But a cutter', he went on, 'must be snug and not sparred like a racing vessel (for cruising).' He liked the appearance of a yacht with the boom overhanging the taffrail. Because if it did not and the bowsprit chopped likewise, the cutter rig 'would be outraged'. The outward appearance of a vessel was much more important before the First War than it was after the Second.

Dixon Kemp thought little of the ketch on the grounds of comfort at sea, remarking that 'owing to the narrowness of the mainsail, there is no rig, area for area, that yields such a healing moment as does the ketch rig'.

He was convinced that the schooner rig was right for the larger vessel, being easy and handy. In bad weather the schooner could be reduced to main trisail, reefed fore staysail and fourth jib with the foresails stowed.

There was, however, a problem that clinched matters when deciding whether to have a cutter or a yawl of 80 tons when cruising. This was the important matter of small boat work. Dixon Kemp looked at it this way. It took four men to row a gig and as there were likely to be six able seamen on a cutter and the same number in a yawl of 80 tons, only two would be left aboard with the captain and mate. It would not be prudent, he said, to manage a 100 ton cutter in a breeze with only four men, though this could be achieved with a yawl of the same size.

With this in mind, the right rig for cruising was a cutter up to 80 tons, a yawl from 80 to 140 tons and a schooner beyond that.

With yachts of 300 tons or 120′ in length or over, the schooner should have three masts. This further divided the rig and made for easy management. Square rig on the foremast in such a vessel is generally recommended, as square topsails may be 'of occasional use in backing and boxhauling', the latter, a method of wearing in bad weather conditions when the size of the sea made it unwise for her to tack. These sails were also useful in scudding in a heavy weather when small trisails set on the lower masts might be becalmed whilst the vessel dropped between the crest of two heavy seas.

The Steam Auxiliary

The problem with vessels of over 300 tons was that though they gave proper accommodation below and avoided the owner 'going on his marrow bones to shave', they were unhandy in narrow channels and crowded roadsteads, like Cowes during The Week. This difficulty produced the need for the 'iron topsail' or auxiliary steam engine. This was easily the most expensive solution, though, for there had to be a permanent crew large enough to work the vessel under sail and the space set aside for boiler, engine and bunkers required the yacht to be lengthened, so increasing the size of the hull and rig needed to make her efficient when under sail alone. There were ingenious devices for overcoming

H.M.S. DAEDALUS and the sea serpent, after Captain M'Quhae's description, South Atlantic 1848. Lt. Edgar Drummond R.N., later to own the yacht BRUNETTE R.Y.S., was officer of the watch. (Cadland Archives)

propeller drag and interference with the rig such as the means of raising the screw and lowering the funnel, for the latter was in the way of the fore or main boom. Such devices were common in the Royal Navy and the remains can be seen on HMS WARRIOR (built 1860) and HMS GANNET (built 1878), owned today by the Maritime Trust.

Even so, the sailing auxiliary, represented by SUNBEAM and VALHALLA, was among the few large yachts to break away from the Baltic, the Channel and the Mediterranean, the popular and fashionable European cruising grounds of the late 19th century, to sail around the world. SUNBEAM is described in some detail in Chapter VI. It is worth looking at VALHALLA, perhaps the finest of this class of vessel, to see how they operated.

VALHALLA, 1,490 tons T.M., was designed by W.C. Storey for Captain J.F. Laycock, later Brigadier Sir Joseph Laycock, and built by Ramage & Ferguson of Leith in 1892. She was one of the very few fully rigged steam yachts and the best example of the steam auxiliary ever built. VALHALLA was magnificent, having an overall length of 245', only 35' shorter than the clipper CUTTY SARK which can be seen at Greenwich. VALHALLA's auxiliary power consisted of a triple expansion steam engine fed by two low pressure Scotch boilers. Her Bevis propeller reduced drag while sailing and this design of screw did much to make the auxiliary popular. The combination of a slow revolving engine and low pressure boilers enabled the maximum number of nautical miles to be covered under power without the need for bunkering. The usual home trade cruising grounds and the Mediterranean were well supplied with coal, but the out of the way places that SUNBEAM, VALHALLA and their ilk wished to visit, were often without any supplies at all. Most of the voyage was, therefore, achieved under sail alone and the design and rig had to reflect this need. The machinery must also be well within the competence of the ship's engineers, both to maintain and, in the case of breakdown, repair.

Captain Laycock cruised in her extensively, going to the Black Sea and calling on the way to take aboard a pipe of port, to help in its improvement. Port was shipped round the world before sale, as it was held that the constant shaking about did much to mature the wine.

VALHALLA continued the glories of her name under the ownership of the Earl of Crawford, who made much use of her between 1902 and 1908. He was a man of remarkable talents and superb appearance. A 'planet struck face' were the words used in the 'Further Memorials of the Royal Yacht Squadron'. This term of affection may come from his appearance or dilection, for he was a noted astronomer. 'The Further Memorials' record that on one fine summer's night 'when several members were drinking their coffee on the battery after dinner, Lord Crawford pointed to a star and said "some day that star may run into the earth". "I hope to God" exclaimed Sir Hercules Langrishe, "we shall be on the starboard tack!"'

Lord Crawford was an ornithologist as well as an astronomer. In pursuit of astronomy, he erected an observatory near Aberdeen and became President of the Royal Astronomical Society, as well as a Fellow of the Royal Society. Indeed, one of his principal reasons for owning VALHALLA was for naturalising and for astronomical observation and he altered her substantially for those purposes. Lord Crawford himself, however, did not put it that way, for in an introductory note to 'Three Voyages of a Naturalist' by M.J. Nicholl, an account of VALHALLA's voyages, he explained:

M.J. Nicholl's drawing of the sea serpent seen from the decks of VALHALLA R.Y.S., in 1905. (Three Voyages of a Naturalist)

> 'For many years it has been my lot to live in close communion with two inseparable hangers-on – the one rheumatism, the other asthma. I found relief by going to sea, provided it was toward the sunny south. The cold and damp of a home winter I have not faced for 15 years.'

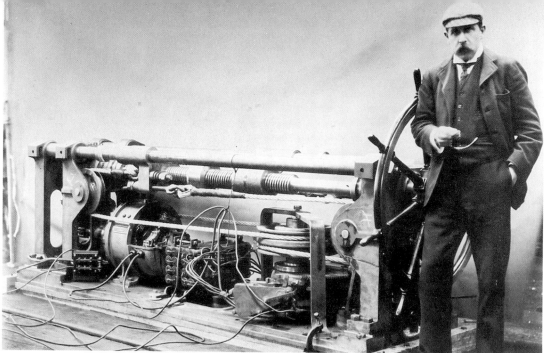

The Earl of Crawford and Balcarres – a man of remarkable talents and superb appearance. VALHALLA which had every modern aid, including electric steering gear, shown with the foreman engineer who built it. (Royal Yacht Squadron and David Couling)

For all this, he braved the rains of Smythes Channel, west of the Magellan Straits. Nicholl records that the magnificent scenery could hardly be appreciated because of the 'execrable climate of this part of the world'. When ashore, they wandered through dripping forests 'water falling from trees, and bushes, the discomfort was great'. However, Lord Crawford seems to have endured that weather without complaint.

Nicholl records how VALHALLA's crew traded with the Fuegians exchanging biscuits, tobacco and matches, in return for 'well worn otter skins with which they were clothed'. Apparently they gave rich reward for these cast-offs and everyone was happy.

This snippet was from the first of VALHALLA's four voyages between 1902 and 1908. Nicholl only recorded three of them, as he was appointed second in charge of the Zoological Gardens at Giza near Cairo in 1907, where he no doubt saw MAHROUSSA, the Egyptian royal yacht, 42 years old even at that date.

The second voyage from December 1903 to May 1904, took in the West Indies and the Cayman Islands. Three new species of birds were discovered during this cruise.

The third voyage reached over to St. Paul's Rocks on the South American side of mid-Atlantic, a VALHALLA favourite, as they had been there on the previous voyage in December 1902.

On December 7th, 1905, some 14 miles off Para on the coast of Brazil, Lord Crawford became the second published member of the Royal Yacht Squadron to see and record a sea serpent. Lt. Edgar Drummond was Officer of the Watch on Her Majesty's Frigate DAEDALUS when on August 6th, 1848 in latitude 24° 44 mins. south, longitude 9° 22 mins. east, he and Mr William Barrett, the Master, saw 'an enormous serpent, with head and shoulders kept about 4' constantly above the surface of the sea, and as nearly as we could approximate, by comparing it with the length of what our main topsail yard would show in the water, there was at very least 60' of the animal, a *fleur d'eau*.

VALHALLA proceeded to South Trinidad, where they discovered the white tern (*gygis crawfordii*), continuing to South Africa, the Seychelles and back to Cowes via the Suez Canal. VALHALLA's fourth voyage was to the Far East.

NORSEMAN R.Y.S. owned by the Earl of Londsdale, designed by St. Clare Byrne, a master of the larger auxiliary steam yacht. (Beken of Cowes)

In the first of these voyages, VALHALLA covered 72,000 nautical miles. Nicholl records that her steam engine drove her at a speed of 10½-11 knots in favourable conditions, while under sail the ship could clip along at 16 knots. VALHALLA had a crew of 65, including officers, engineers and stewards. The accommodation was palatial, with electric light throughout. She also had a freezing room and so carried many tons of meat, sufficient for long cruises. She was one of the first yachts to be so fitted which was prophetic, as this splendid yacht ended her days as a Spanish refrigerated fruit carrier, foundering off Cape St. Vincent in 1922.

But to return to Lord Crawford's ownership, on the third voyage, two days out of Durban, VALHALLA was caught in a cyclone and justified Nicholl's claim that 'a better sea boat has probably never been built'. The ship was hove to and he vividly recorded the scene through the eyes of a naturalist:

> 'Distinguishing above the roaring of the wind and the tumult of the breaking seas, we could hear the wild cries of whimbrels and great numbers of other wading birds, and terns could be seen flying round the ship. At early dawn a tern was blown against the rigging, so fiercely, that one of its wings was completely ripped away.'

Lord Crawford used his yacht in the manner of Prince Albert of Monaco, employing her as a research vessel. This did not prevent him, however, from engaging in the frivolity of yacht racing, for in August 1902 he presented the Squadron with the Coronation Cup. This was for auxiliary steam vessels of over 340 tons T.M. and upwards, engines not to be used except to come up to the line and then only 30 minutes before the start. There can have been few more splendid sights than the line between St. Helen's Fort and the Nab on August 18th that year, until the gatherings of the training ships and the Sail Training Association's 'Tall Ship Races' of the last two decades. The competitors in the Coronation Cup were Lord Brassey's CZARINA, 564 tons, Mr Allison Armour's schooner UTOWANA, 560 tons, Mr John Fergusson's schooner ROSABELLE, 439 tons and, of course, VALHALLA. The course was to Cherbourg, back round the Eddystone Light, and thence east to the Squadron Line. CZARINA went aground at the start and UTOWANA, the only pure fore and after, won easily.

In 1905 VALHALLA took part in the German Emperor's Ocean Cup Race from Sandy Hook to the Lizard, coming third.

Another particularly beautiful example of the auxiliaries was NORSEMAN. This three masted barquentine followed the classic line of the clipper. The term 'clipper' came from 'clip', to move quickly, and became applied to fast sailing vessels. The clipper bow and counter stern became, with a sleek hull in between, the identifying feature of the clipper and the ideal for those who wished for a palace at sea, with both sea-keeping ability and speed. Such ships as the American clipper SOVEREIGN OF THE SEAS, built in 1852 by Donald McKay which managed to log 22 knots, at times, in her record 13 days 22 hours from New York to Liverpool, gave the clipper ship great appeal. The hull profile, above the water at any rate, was adopted, with modifications, by most auxiliaries and many large pure steam yachts. Indeed, this elegant and classic line was carried right through into the design of later motor-powered pleasure vessels.

NORSEMAN, 521 tons, was designed by St. Clare Byrne, who had been responsible for Lord Brassey's SUNBEAM. She was built of steel by D. & W. Henderson & Co. of Glasgow, in 1898, for S.R. Platt. NORSEMAN was 160′ in length and had a beam of 27′ with a draught of 15′ 6″. Her owner sold her to the 5th Earl of Lonsdale (1857-1944) in 1906. The Yellow

The schooner VERENA on which the Yellow Earl wore the flago of the Vice Admiral of the Cumberland Fleet and confused the membership of the Squadron. (Beken of Cowes)

Mr Albert Brassey's CZARINA R.Y.S., which competed in the Coronation Cup Race of 1902 for auxiliary steam vessels. Brassey's brother was the owner of SUNBEAM. (Beken of Cowes)

Earl, as he was known, had been elected to the Royal Yacht Squadron in 1894. His passage into the Club was typical of his larger than life behaviour. His elder brother, St. George, the 4th Earl, died in 1881. He had been the owner of the steam yacht NORTHUMBRIA and the schooner HORNET and had been a member of the Squadron himself. This did not smooth the way for brother Hugh, who knew that his election would be a difficult one and determined on a course that would have been fatal to anyone else.

He knew that the Club, with their close relationship with the Royal Navy, were against rejecting Admirals and so he arrived in Cowes Roads with a Vice-Admiral's flag, which much resembled the Vice-Commodore's pennant, at the masthead of his schooner VERENA.

When he landed, he pointed out that as hereditary Vice-Admiral of the Cumberland Coast, he was entitled to wear it. Members were stunned by this act of bravado and he was elected. Douglas Sutherland, in his amusing biography 'The Yellow Earl', points out the beauty of this strategy, for the office of Vice-Admiral of the Cumberland Coast was not hereditary at all, but in the gift of the Monarch. On the death of his brother, the Queen had not honoured Hugh but his neighbour, Lord Hothfield of Appleby Castle.

Two years later, his bold ways were to bring more attention, for in 1895, while he was acting as sailing master to the Kaiser, the 80th anniversary of the Royal Yacht Squadron was being celebrated by the commissioning of a massed portrait of members. Strict form was observed and those nearest the Prince of Wales and the Emperor of Germany were the most senior, tailing off to the very junior, scattered in front of the Castle Wall and on the battlements.

Lord Lonsdale was senior in age and companionship, but very junior by date of election, for he had only been a member for one year. Seniority, therefore, should have only allowed him to peep at the Prince and His Imperial Highness. This was not good enough for the 5th Earl and he approached the artist from the firm of Dickinson's and explained his friendship with the Prince and the Emperor, suggesting that it would be much better if he were placed in that little group. The artist complied, to the horror of those present at the unveiling. The Earl of Lonsdale was painted out by order of the Committee and re-emerged in another part of the canvas, still appearing senior.

Perhaps this is why the authors of the 'Memorials of the Royal Yacht Squadron', Montague Guest and William Boulton commented – 'Lord Lonsdale, the finished horseman, grand whip and good all round sportsman who seems of late to have rather cooled in his former ardour for the sea'. They were writing soon after this experience, for he had certainly regained some of his enthusiasm in becoming the owner of NORSEMAN, one of the most attractive yachts ever seen in Cowes Roads, though he sold her three years later.

The Steam Yacht

The attitude of the Yacht Club, later the Squadron, to the steam yacht in the early days and the Club's treatment of Thomas Ashetton-Smith as a result, has been mentioned in the preceding chapter. The reason for this early opposition was, as has been noted, that engines did nothing to improve the sailing vessel or seamanship. The aversion, though, by yachtsmen generally was broader than this. Smoke, coal dust and waste of space were the three factors against steam in contemporary eyes. This objection was held by many until the coming of the internal combustion engine.

Robert Napier first made a success of the idea of placing a kettle in a boat, in ROB ROY, after a commission had been given to him by Henry Bell, the Glasgow developer. Napier's fame, however, came from LEVEN ·in 1823. In 1827, the Royal Northern Yacht Club presented a cup for a Clyde Steamer Race from Rothesay to Great Cumbrae and back to the start. Napier swept the board with CLARENCE winning and HELENBURG coming a close second. It was at this point that Thomas Ashetton-Smith of Tedworth took an interest and asked Napier to come and see him. At Andover he explained what he wanted. He told not only of the Yacht Club's dislike of steam yachts, but the similar feelings of his wife. Ashetton-Smith relied on Napier to persuade the latter before he could give an order. As has already been seen, Napier must have made a good impression on Mrs Ashetton-Smith, for he and his client were really responsible for the development of the steam yacht. By 1839 Ashetton-Smith felt confident enough to issue a challenge that FIRE KING would beat all comers – the wager being £5,000. The good lady, too, must have made a favourable impression on Napier, for he gave her a water engine to blow the organ at Tedworth.

Erik Hoffman, in his notable work 'The Steam Yachts', traces the growth of steam powered pleasure at sea through the Yacht Registers. There were only 30 powered by steam in 1863, 140 in 1873 and 466 in 1883. The number dropped to 263 in 1913, just before the First War, as the diesel began to provide a less space-hungry and cleaner alternative.

In 1868, the second steamer race was held, this time at Cowes. The competition was between CORNELIA, of 305 tons owned by Lord Vane, later the Marquess of Londonderry and EÖTHEN, 345 tons, belonging to Mr Talbot. The prize was £100 but it is not recorded who won. *Bells Life* was scathing about the idea, observing 'this can hardly be considered an improvement on the Squadron programme'.

The epic voyage of the steam yacht FOX was quite another matter and her part in discovering what happened to the Arctic explorer, Sir John Franklin (1786-1847), is an epic, perhaps without parallel, in the history of yachts.

FOX, a screw steamer of 300 tons T.M., 177 tons burden, was built by Messrs. Hall & Co. of Aberdeen for Sir Richard Sutton, the 3rd Baronet, in the early 1850s. Sir Richard was the first of three famous Sutton baronets, all named Richard, and all members of the Squadron, who took a great interest in yachting. The 5th Baronet was a member of the Royal Thames and challenged for the America's Cup, with GENESTA. The start of the first race in this series was celebrated, for GENESTA poked her bowsprit, with the benefit of right of way, through the mainsail of the American defender PURITAN. But to return to FOX and Sir Richard Sutton, 3rd Baronet.

The photograph, shows FOX *beset in the ice, June 1858. Taken by David Walker, surgeon and naturalist.* (Scott Polar Research Institute)

Lady Franklin's steam yacht FOX, *commanded by Captain Francis McClintock R.N., searching for Sir John Franklin and the crews of H.M.S.'s* EREBUS *and* TERROR. *The sailing Master for this successful expedition was Captain Allen Young R.N.R.* (National Maritime Museum)

According to records, he joined the Squadron with FOX, cruised to Norway in her and then died, all in the year 1855. Lady Franklin bought FOX from Sir Richard's executors in 1857 for £2,000 and gave command to Captain F.L. McClintock ((1819-1907), later Admiral Sir Francis McClintock, KCB, FRS.

There were 39 expeditions in all to try and discover what had happened to Franklin and his two ships, HMS EREBUS and HMS TERROR when they failed to return from a quest to find the legendary North-West Passage. Sir John had left Britain on May 19th, 1845. He and his ships were spotted on July 26th at the head of Baffin Bay. Since that sighting, nothing more was heard or seen of them. There was considerable interest in both Britain and America in trying to ascertain exactly what had happened to them. Jane, Lady Franklin, Sir John's second wife, spared neither energy nor pennies in her search for the truth. The yacht FOX was part of this herculean effort.

To this end FOX was stripped of all finery. McClintock describes the meaning of the refit for the ice in his book 'The Fate of Sir John Franklin' published in 1859.

> 'The velvet hangings and splendid furniture of the yacht, and also everything not contributing part of the vessel's strengthening were to be removed; the large skylights and capacious ladderways had to be reduced to limits more adapted to a polar clime; the whole vessel to be externally sheathed with stout planking, and internally fortified by strong cross beams, longitudinal beams, iron stanchions and diagonal fastenings; the false keel taken off, the slender brass propeller replaced by a massive iron one, the boiler taken out, altered, and enlarged; the sharp stem to be cased in iron until it resembled a ponderous chisel set up edgeways; even the yacht's rig had to be altered.'

FOX was fitted out with 'the strictest economy' and officers 'crammed into pigeon holes, styled cabins, in order to make room for provisions and stores'. McClintock notes that the officers' 'mess room, for five persons, measured 8′ square'.

73

Sir Allen Young 'perhaps the best and most competent sailorman who has ever flown the Squadron flag'. (Royal Yacht Squadron)

Provisioning was very different to that required for FOX when Sir Richard took her to Norway as a base for salmon fishing. McClintock required enough lemon juice and pickles for a daily ration for each of the 26 crew for 28 months, as well as as much of Messrs. Allsopp's ale 'as we can find room for'.

6,682lbs of pemmican were provided by the Royal Clarence Victualling Yard at Gosport for this Arctic expedition. Pemmican was composed of prime beef, cut into thin slices and dried over a wood fire; then pounded up and mixed with about an equal weight of beef fat, all pressed into cases of 42lbs each.

The yachting fraternity were interested in the voyage and Captain McClintock was elected a member of the Royal Harwich Yacht Club and presented with their burgee. The Royal Victoria Yacht Club at Ryde on the Isle of Wight invited him to join them as well. On his departure he was elected a member of the Royal Yacht Squadron.

FOX sailed as planned for the Artic on July 1st, 1857. Lady Franklin had said in her instructions to Captain McClintock that she had 'unbounded confidence' in him. This must have been reinforced by the knowledge that Captain Allen W. Young of the Mercantile Marine was in the position of sailing master, of whom more later.

McClintock and the crew of the FOX discovered in their two years in the Arctic most of what is known about the fate of Franklin and his men. They found a cairn in which was buried a log of the fated expedition up to April 25th, 1848. This showed that Sir John was near to discovering the North-West Passage through Peel Sound, when they were trapped by the ice off King William Island. Franklin died aboard ship with a number of his men, through scurvy, and the remainder perished in an attempt to reach safety over the ice, some 18 months after being first beset. The FOX returned with this information to the Thames, calling at Portsmouth on September 21st, 1859 to drop the captain.

McClintock's crew learnt many things aboard FOX, one of the most valuable being how to live together. This lesson is still best learnt in a small boat and FOX was small for 26 men. McClintock wrote in the conclusion of his book, when remembering the gold watch his crew had given him: 'As long as I live it will remind me of that perfect harmony, that mutual esteem and goodwill, which made our ship's company a happy little community, and contributed materially to the success of the expedition.'

Captain McClintock was knighted in 1860, the year after his account of the voyage was published and he ended up as Commander-in-Chief West Indies Station, all after a remarkable voyage in a yacht.

A word now about his sailing master. He was the Sir Allen Young mentioned in Chapter II who was dining with Sir Percy Shelley at the Squadron when the 'Pirate' threatened to bombard the Castle at Cowes.

Allen Young had entered the merchant service in 1846 and had command of the East Indiaman MARLBOROUGH, of 1,500 tons, on two world voyages during the years 1853 and 1854. On one of these he bet £1,000 that he would deliver the Calcutta mails in London first. He made Weymouth, his port, dined at the Gloucester Hotel, drove to Dorchester, caught the train and reached London 12 hours before his rival, who had chosen Liverpool. Captain Young was the master of the steam trooper ADELAIDE of 3,000 tons during the Crimean War, before joining FOX as sailing master. He later commanded the latter as part of the North Atlantic Telegraph expedition of 1862. Apart from being a Lieutenant in the Royal Naval Reserve, he commanded the QUANTUNG of the Chinese European Navy from 1862 to 1864, during the Taeping Rebellion.

Arctic Yacht PANDORA R.Y.S., owned by Sir Allen Young, a veteran of the search for Franklin. PANDORA made two further voyages in search of more information, following the FOX expedition.
(Beken of Cowes)

Captain Young was haunted by the feeling that there were more Franklin records to be found, in particular the journals of HMS EREBUS and TERROR. These would complete the picture sketched in by the successful FOX expedition. In order to fulfill this ambition and being of independent means, he bought the Royal Naval five gun sloop PANDORA of 430 tons burden. She had been built at Devonport in 1863 and had assisted in a punitive expedition against the Congo pirates in 1868. PANDORA was built for speed under sail or steam. Messrs. Day, Summers & Co. of Southampton had the job of preparing her for the Arctic. Rigged as a barquentine, she carried eight boats, including a steam cutter.

The expedition was carried out under the burgee of the Royal Yacht Squadron and its purpose was to visit the western coast of Greenland, thence to proceed through Baffin's Sea, Lancaster Sound and Barrow Strait, toward the magnetic pole and, if practicable, to navigate through the North-West Passage to the Pacific. On passing King William Island, they were to look for further records, including the journals of the two ships of Franklin's expedition. However, in the event, PANDORA did not reach further than the Franklin Strait between Prince of Wales Island and North Somerset because of an impenetrable barrier of ice. They visited Beechey Island though, and found Northumberland House looking a bit sad. This wooden hut had been built by Commander Pullen of the NORTH STAR in the autumn of 1852 from the lower masts and spars of the American whaler M'LELLAN, which had been crushed in the ice of Melville Bay in the same year. Alongside the building was the cutter MARY, 12 tons, in good condition. She had been towed out by the 91 ton schooner FELIX as part of Sir John Ross's expedition in 1850. Northumberland

House had been broken into and ransacked. Allen Young suspected bears. In 'The Two Voyages of PANDORA', published in 1879, he wrote: 'A cask of rum standing in the doorway, intact, was conclusive proof to my mind that neither eskimo or British sailors had entered that way.'

The Arctic yacht PANDORA R.Y.S. returned home, entering the Channel on October 14th in gale conditions – 'We sent down the topgallant yards and got the funnel up and screw down, and lighted fires, but continued under canvas, and anchored at Spithead at daylight on the 16th October, 1875.'

PANDORA had one more attempt the following year at navigating the North-West Passage, but ended up, because of very difficult ice conditions, pushing north to Smith's Channel between Greenland and Ellesmere Island. She was nearly crushed in the ice in so doing. PANDORA was back at Portsmouth by November 3rd, 1876. Captain Allen Young was knighted soon after and his parties aboard his steam yacht STELLA, of 169 tons, became famous, no doubt illuminated by his sea experience. Indeed, 'The Memorials' remember him as 'perhaps the best and most competent sailorman who has ever flown the Squadron flag.'

No doubt Sir Allen would have agreed that the essence of yachting, whether under sail or steam, was the pleasure that the pastime was able to give and the steam yacht was conceived in order to maximise this and reduce the moments when weather or lack of achievement to windward, became oppressive.

One of the great exponents of pleasure aboard steam yachts, properly employed, was W.J. Pawson, who owned the steam yacht EUPHROSYNE, built at Gosport in 1889, the year her owner joined the Squadron. EUPHROSYNE was of 223 tons and 130' overall. This beautiful steam yacht was designed by C.E. Nicholson and built by his celebrated firm, Camper & Nicholson. William Pawson and EUPHOSYNE, together with his friends, either aboard his, or on their own yachts, would assemble at Cowes when prawns were in season. For several weeks they would eat little else and because of this habit were known as 'the prawn eaters'.

Others, too, were famous for their parties afloat, notably His Excellency & Madame de Falbe aboard CHAZALIE of 528 tons and Sir Edward and Lady Guinness, later the Earl and Countess of Iveagh, on CETONIA, a schooner of classic lines of 203 tons.

In the latter part of the 19th century, the steam yacht followed the example of the sailing vessel that cruised, in providing a special ladies' cabin. Claud Worth, writing before the First War, indicated that sailing yachts under 50' were unsuitable for cruising with the female sex aboard because the ladies could not be guaranteed the right measure of privacy. Modern experience, using his terms, has yet, perhaps, to disprove this. It was not only sight but sound, as illustrated by a limerick composed by A. Briscoe in 1912:

> 'There was a young girl called Bianca,
> Asleep on a ship while at anchor;
> But she awoke in dismay,
> When she heard the mate say,
> Let's haul up the top'sheet and spanker.'

The cruise of the cutter GANYMEDE related in Chapter II tells of the ladies' cabin aboard a sailing yacht and the strange noises that disturbed Mrs Condy and her friends.

A look at the accommodation plan of MAID OF HONOUR, built by Day, Summers & Co. of Southampton for the Earl of Cawdor in 1891, shows a typical layout for a steam yacht of

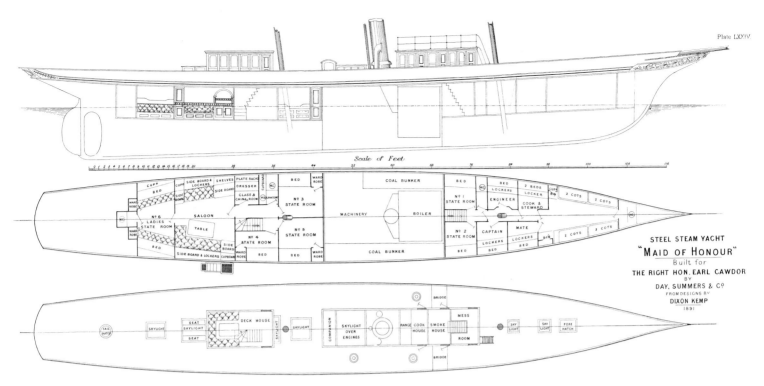

Plate LXXIV

Scale of Feet

STEEL STEAM YACHT
"MAID OF HONOUR"
Built for
THE RIGHT HON. EARL CAWDOR
BY
DAY, SUMMERS & Cº
FROM DESIGNS BY
DIXON KEMP
1891

The steel steam yacht MAID OF HONOUR I built by Day, Summers and Co. for the Earl of Cawdor in 1891 to the designs of Dixon Kemp. The ladies' cabin was aft in a prime position later occupied by the owner and his wife. (National Maritime Museum)

182 tons T.M. MAID OF HONOUR's other dimensions were 126′ 8″ length overall, 17′ 7″ beam and a draught of 11′ 1″. The yacht had auxiliary sails and was to the design of Dixon Kemp.

The ladies' cabin was aft in a prime position, later usually occupied by the owner and his wife. In the long, thin yachts of the period and of this comparatively small size, the propeller was well aft of the accommodation and so this important cabin was relatively free of propeller noise and vibration. The screw would also be turning at low revolutions under steam power and there would have been remarkably little reason to notice the engine. Motive power would have been like the wind, if it had not been for the smoke, smuts and coal dust, which were present, even with the best engineers, at times.

On Lord Cavan's yacht, the ladies had their own water closet and their cabin gave out into the saloon, in which breakfast, lunch and dinner were served, unless weather encouraged meals to be taken in the deckhouse above.

The crew had their mess room under the bridge. The smokehouse immediately abaft was again for the crew, for many owners were against men smoking in the fo'c'sle or on deck. Dixon Kemp recommended that 'smoking should be permitted on the fore deck for a half hour after breakfast and dinner; also during dog watches, (the two hour first and last "dog" between 4 p.m. and 8 p.m.,) and in the first watch (midnight to four) if the men so please; and the men are sometimes allowed a pipe in the morning at eleven o'clock as "lunch".'

MAID OF HONOUR was later owned by William K. Millar, brother of the owner of the ketch CARIAD I. He built a second twin screw steam driven MAID OF HONOUR (later SYLVANA) of 487 tons T.M. in Lord Ailsa's Ailsa Shipbuilding Company, at Troon in 1907. The new yacht was some 50′ longer and W.K. Millar made extensive use of her, cruising to Norway after the salmon and into the sun of the Mediterranean.

MAID OF HONOUR II R.Y.S. moored in Norwegian waters. She was built in 1907 by the Ailsa Shipbuilding Co. (John Millar)

Many yachtsmen, particularly those with comfortably large vessels, used to make good use of their yachts in this way. Norway was a favourite place and some liked fishing so much that they bought or leased the fishing rights, returning year after year with a party, very often made up of the same people. Gentlemen well versed in the art of fishing and, indeed, shooting, found the yacht a valuable aid. A.G. Bagot, himself an owner of a steam yacht, was a keen shot and an experienced sailor. He was also an author, writing under the name of 'Bagatelle'. One of his works was full of practical hints to yachtsmen, entitled 'Shooting & Yachting in the Mediterranean', specifically aimed at those who wished to do more than 'sight-see' or enjoy the sun.

He included in his hunting grounds the Greek and Albanian coasts, across from the island of Corfu. His yacht would lie securely at anchor there, while the steam launch, towing the Berthon collapsible boat, would venture over to the eastern shore. Bagot's chief steward used to man the latter, for he was a first rate shot. On one occasion they 'folded' the boat and launched it on an inland lake, the steward armed with an eight bore shoulder gun. So equipped, he pushed off from the shore in the Berthon boat and stalked a large raft of ducks, watched by his employer and friends who were loaded and ready for birds that he disturbed – 'Up got the duck', Bagot recalls, 'Boom went the gun, head over heels backwards went the steward into the boat, which being a light cockle shell, turned nearly over, and half filled with water, the result of all this being one duck floating dead on top of the water.'

Apart from many reminiscences, Bagot gives harbour information amply spiced with sporting notes. At Dragomastre in Greece, for example, he observes:

> '*Sport* – Excellent woodcock-shooting close by at Petela, where there is good anchorage in 4 fathoms, and all round the foot of the hills. Red deer and wild boar, duck, and a most prolific cave full of blue-rock pigeons, which affords capital sport. The cave is about three miles from the anchorage, off the second bluff on the starboard hand going out. The country is not altogether safe, as the populace are a cut-throat-looking community, and not above a bit of brigandage. It is as well to be cautious, and to go out a large party.'

MAID OF HONOUR II fitting out at the Ailsa Shipbuilding Company at Troon. (John Millar)

A contemporary postcard of Monte Carlo harbour before the breakwater was built. Prince Albert's yacht PRINCESSE ALICE is in the foreground. (Cadland Archives)

The steam yacht ABONA, a typical gentleman's steam yacht of the smaller size that cruised the ports of Europe. (Steele Collection)

For Monte Carlo, he is a little terse, as sporting facilities seem to have been entirely lacking.

> 'MONACO – Unsafe to lie in a sailing vessel. Anchor off Gas-works, and keep steam.
> *Hotel* – Grand Hotel, Monte Carlo.'

Under 'Conclusion', however, 'Bagatelle' is more informative and amongst a mass of recipes and useful hints, there are at least two which are still to be recommended for the butt or for yachts under steam or sail.

> 'A Good Drink to Shoot on.
>
> Have the bottles filled with cold tea; into each quart of tea squeeze the juice of 2 lemons or 4 limes, and 1 gill of whisky; no sugar or milk.
>
> 'A "Pick Me Up."
>
> Beat up the yolk of one egg in a tumbler of milk, add a wine-glass of sherry, 2 grains of Quinine, 10 drops of Jamaica ginger, a dessertspoonful of sugar, and half a glass of brandy. This makes enough for two people.'

Erik Hoffman in 'The Steam Yachts' records how game used to be displayed to friends and rivals on other vessels, by hoisting the 'larder' on a line like signal flags.

ABONA, of 123 tons T.M., built by Lobnitz of Renfrew on the Clyde, a yard that vied with the Ailsa Shipbuilding Company, was typical of the smaller-sized gentleman's steam yacht that cruised round the ports of Europe.

The photograph shows her during her time with H.D.H. Crosse, who owned her from 1906 to 1908.

TITANIA was a good example of the range of steam yachts built by Day, Summers & Co. The beauty of the hull, with the fine sheer reaching up to the bow and more subtly toward the taffrail, is the height of elegance. (Steele collection)

Lord Dunraven aboard GRIANAIG R.Y.S. when a hospital ship during the First World War. In his youth he had to choose between the fiddle string and the tarry rope. He chose the latter. (Radio Times Hulton Picture Library)

One of the finest yards at the turn of the century was Day, Summers & Co. They turned out a particularly beautiful range of small steam yachts at Southampton. Lord Cawdor's MAID OF HONOUR was built by them. Another example of their craftsmanship was TITANIA. She was some 10′ shorter and a foot less in the beam and draught, and was owned in 1924 by Sir Richard Williams Bulkeley, Bart., Commodore of the Royal Yacht Squadron at that time.

The beauty of the hull with the fine sheer reaching up to the bow and more subtly toward the taffrail is the height of elegance. The bowsprit is correctly mounted so that it butts against the fo'c'sle and is visibly supported by the stem and the gilded trail boards. This care in design shows pure-blooded descent from the clipper, unlike so many awkward modern copies, where the designer has little idea what he is about.

The teak-panelled deck houses, open bridge, raked masts, yellow funnel with its top parallel to the sheer and ensign staff similarly parallel to the counter's transom were what made the vessel such a delight to the eye. The scrubbed canvas mast coat on the mizzen, stained by smoke, shows that she had been under weigh for an hour or two. In harbour this would have been scrubbed and clayed white again.

The sail covers are spotless too. Such attention to detail was typical of the classic pleasure yachts of the period and followed the traditions of the Royal yachts of the last three quarters of the 19th century. TITANIA's sailing ship hull and comparatively deep draught would have made her sea kindly and comfortable to live on

GRIANAIG, (coming from *Grianair* – to bask in the sun. *Grianan* is less appropriate – a dry place for peats) followed the same line but was much larger, reaching 168′ overall and having a Thames tonnage of 439. She was owned between 1906 and 1912 by Bend'or, Duke of Westminster. The Duke sold her to buy BELEM (Bethlehem), a clipper, built in 1896 to carry cocoa beans from Para, Brazil to Nantes. He converted her to a yacht in 1918, selling her to Colonel the Hon. Arthur Guinness who renamed her FANTOME II. She later became an Italian training ship operating out of Venice and was renamed GIORGIO CINI. The Duke of Westminster continued his yachting career after the First War with two FLYING CLOUDS of 1087 and 1195 tons respectively and the converted destroyer CUTTY SARK.

The Earl of Dunraven became the next owner of GRIANAIG and he bought, commanded and maintained her, at his own expense, during the First War as a hospital ship in both the Channel and the Mediterranean. He was 73 years old when he conceived the idea.

The 3rd Earl of Dunraven (1812-1896) was particularly gifted. He was an artist and an accomplished musician. 'The sea', he recorded, 'was the master passion, and one fine day I had to come to a momentous decision – the violin requires suppleness and delicacy of hands and fingers, and handling ropes, rowing, and other outdoor games and sports are incompatible with that necessary condition. It was not easy to decide; but, after a struggle, the tarry rope beat the fiddle string, and I have never touched the violin again.' He won the King's Cup with CARIAD II, as has been mentioned, in 1905, 1912 and 1921, as well as the Queen's Cup, and challenged for the America's Cup in 1893 and 1895 with VALKYRIE II and III. In the last of these challenges Dunraven was against the American yacht DEFENDER, again skippered by the redoubtable 'Hank' Haff, who had defeated William Henn and GALATEA. Lord Dunraven was beaten and much aggrieved. He accused the Americans of increasing their waterline length overnight by adding extra ballast. In the third race, he retired after crossing the starting line because of the behaviour of the

PAMPA, later JOYANCE, a steam yacht designed by Charlie Nicholson, had red leather buttoned seats and mahogany furniture in the deck saloon. The only disturbing feature in the photograph is the way the telescopes are stored without their protective caps on the shelf in the right foreground. (Beken of Cowes)

spectator fleet. This last complaint was not upheld and the race went to the DEFENDER. The antics of the onlookers have been a worry ever since. His charge of cheating by adding ballast was found, by an inquiry, to be without foundation. Life aboard GRIANAIG, therefore, even during the War, must have been peaceful compared with these wrangles.

Steam yachts reached a magnificence that is difficult now to contemplate. It was not only the elegance of profile but the richness below which seems quite impossible to envisage at sea today. No-one can look at the outside or inside of such yachts as SEMIRAMIS, ERIN or NARCISSUS, shown in detail in Chapter VI, without wonder. A foretaste of this inside view on a more modest scale is given by PAMPA, later JOYANCE.

PAMPA was comparatively small for those days, being only 225 tons T.M., 103′ 8″ overall, 22′ 9″ beam and 10′ 7″ draught. She was designed by the great Charlie Nicholson and owned by G. Hamilton-Fletcher, who made a habit of having 'Joy' as the first part of his yachts' names. Between 1901 and 1930, he had five, JOYANCE, JOYEEN, JOYETTE, JOYEUSE, and JOYFARER. JOYEUSE played an important part in the dog world, for

Gwendolen Hamilton-Fletcher, later Wingfield-Digby, brought the first Dutch barge dog or Keeshond back to Britain aboard her in 1902. The breed is now internationally recognised. PAMPA was fitted with a four cylinder paraffin motor, which would have given her more room below as there was no need for the stoke hold. The deck saloon, with, no doubt, red leather buttoned seats and mahogany furniture, looked magnificent. The particularly well designed swinging table, screwed to the floor, is a feature, as is the carved companion-way down. The only disturbing feature in the photograph is the way the telescopes are stored, without their protecting caps, on a shelf in the right foreground.

Yacht Racing

The idea that a salt-water palace should be an out and out racing yacht may offend both those who sail to race and those who believe that the competitive use of a yacht destroys many of the joys of going to sea at all. This thought comes from the racing habit of living frugally, in order to cut down weight. Such weight pinching might vary from leaving the piano ashore to counting the number of socks the crew bring aboard. A Scots yachtsman who wrote under the pen name 'The Governor' summarised the racing view in 'A Yachtsman's Holidays' published in 1889.

> 'Yacht racing is no longer a mere pastime, it is a profession and a racing vessel is hardly ever used for pleasure sailing, partly because she is generally rather deficient in the necessary adjuncts to comfort, but chiefly because a racing skipper and his crew would think cruising a sinful waste of time and neglect of opportunities for adding to the prize money.'

The cruising man, on the other hand, may feel that gentlemen do not go to windward, with just the same verve and conviction. It is rather in line with reputed remarks of Lord Curzon, for he said that 'gentlemen do not eat soup for lunch'.

There are, however, shades of opinion and indeed options between leaving the piano or the socks ashore, for there are sailors who are devoted to cruising, yet actually enjoy a thrash into the wind.

Again, there are, or perhaps more accurately were, racing yachts that were of such royal appearance, purpose and achievement that they could be described as salt-water palaces. The racing cutter ARROW must have been one of these.

ARROW was built by Thomas Inman (now the Berthon Boat Company) at Lymington in 1821 for Mr Joseph Weld. She was then a cutter of 84 tons, 61′ 5″ in length and of 18′ 5″ beam, later lengthened and brought up to 117 tons. Her mast was stepped almost amidships and, like most of her contemporaries, she had a straight stem, overhung by a magnificent bowsprit. ARROW had a particularly attractive sheer, unusual for her time. She won the first cup presented by the Royal Yacht Club and the Challenge Trophy given by George IV.

ARROW was one of 15 yachts that took part in the first America's Cup Race in 1851. The prize was presented by the Squadron. She was then under the ownership of Thomas Chamberlayne of Cranbury Park near Winchester, who bought her on December 22nd, 1846 for £116 and retrieved her from a mud berth, where the yacht had been laid up for a number of years.

The course for the race was eastward around the Wight and as they passed Bembridge Ledge, ARROW was in the lead with another British yacht, VOLANTE, lying second. ARROW

ran aground off Ventnor, still leading. The first ALARM, built by Inman in 1830, went to her aid. VOLANTE was the next casualty, for she sprang her bowsprit, so leaving AMERICA in a commanding position, for she finished off the Castle, at Cowes, 21 minutes ahead.

ARROW beat AMERICA in the Queen's Cup race at Ryde in 1852 and so boasted, correctly, that she had never been bettered by the famous schooner. ARROW's navigator for that first race has much to answer for.

ARROW was in commission for 59 years until 1880, when she was broken up. Her owner had a small replica made for the lake at Cranbury Park, and so followed a royal tradition of diminutive yachts on lakes, started by the Sun King.

Perhaps the greatest name in Victorian and Edwardian yacht racing was Archibald Kennedy, the 3rd Marquess of Ailsa. His life spanned the times of the great cutters and schooners of the late 19th and early 20th centuries and he died in 1938 at the age of 90. Lord Ailsa was mourned as the father of modern yachting. His reputation came from a scientific approach to the sport and to fine seamanship. 'The Further Memorials' illustrate this with a story told by Lady Ailsa after his death, remembering SLEUTHHOUND's victory in the race for the King of the Netherlands Cup in 1883.

'When the race day dawned, the wind was southerly, gusting to gale force, with poor visibility. At breakfast an old retainer at the Squadron begged Lord Ailsa not to sail. The great yachtsman, perhaps to change the subject, asked for a pie that was on the breakfast sideboard for his lunch. The retainer replied that it was against the rules to take food out of the dining room, but added, "but you shall have it, and I hope you will live to eat it".'

The great yachtsman survived to beat the large schooners with the comparatively small cutter rigged SLEUTHHOUND, roaring through the fleet toward the end of the race, pushed in a cloud of foam by a 'fierce, dark squall'.

Lord Ailsa's BEAGLE *on the slip of the Culzean Shipbuilding and Engineering Company, then using the boathouse below the great Adam Castle.*
(The Marquess of Ailsa)

Such survival and triumph were the hallmark of his most famous racing yacht BLOODHOUND, or the 'Hound', as she was popularly known. The idea of building her came to Lord Ailsa in 1874 when he was contemplating buying the 60 ton NEVA, the fruits of an executor's sale. He was persuaded by his friends, however, to change course and go for the smaller 40 instead. BLOODHOUND's conception and birth was, therefore, a providence.

In her first year, BLOODHOUND won 11 prizes out of 20 starts and her success continued until the late 70's, when she appeared to be outclassed. In 1880 Lord Ailsa sold her and BLOODHOUND was cruised and raced by various owners, eventually going to the ship breakers for the value of her lead. When Lord Ailsa heard this news he determined to buy her back. He had only eight races, of which four were firsts, out of her when the 'Hound' was sunk in collision with L'ESPERANCE, owned by Prince Henry of Prussia.

Her capacity for survival ensured that she raced again the next year and this she did regularly until she met her end in a fire at White's Yard, Southampton, in 1922. BLOODHOUND was certainly a magnificent racing yacht, perhaps one of the most famous ever built, but hardly a palace below, for when she was launched BLOODHOUND was little more than a shell, having a single seat along each side of the cabin. Lord Ailsa relied for his comfort on his steam yachts. He owned MARCHESA between 1878 and 1880 and TITANIA between 1881 and 1890. Similarly, when he had FOXHOUND in the early 70's, she was paired with the 140 ton schooner, LADY EVELYN.

BLOODHOUND was one of the yachts borne of a remarkable partnership between the two Fifes, William II and III and Lord Ailsa. The Fife designs were not only successful in racing terms but perhaps the best-looking yachts to come from any designer's board, before or since. Lord Ailsa designed small boats himself and had them built in an estate enterprise in the workshops and boathouse of Culzean Castle. He named this little yard The Culzean Shipbuilding & Engineering Company. They built the cutters BEAGLE, 10 tons, COCKER, five tons, and SNARLEYOW, three tons there. The latter was one of the three tonners of the Portsmouth Corinthian Yacht Club, for this was part of the Marquess' support for small class racing, encouraging what became known as the 'Corinthian Spirit'. However, the short beach and the estate workshops at the top of the cliff proved too small and too inconvenient for larger vessels. Materials and gear had to be lowered a couple of hundred feet and ferried to the boathouse. Lord Ailsa moved his enterprise to Maidens, three miles southwest, where there was more room and proper facilities could be provided. The yard was close by Shanter Farm, the traditional home of Burn's Tam O'Shanter. In his poem, Burns describes Nannie pursuing the fleeing Tam on his grey mare Meg, with her outstretched hand grasping the animal's tail. This was the inspiration for the figurehead of the clipper ship CUTTY SARK. Perhaps this spirit made the new yard a success, for it was soon too small, which led to the founding of the Ailsa Shipbuilding Company at Troon, the building place of the Duke of Portland's famous PANTALOON described in Chapter II.

The Ayrshire coast on which the Adam Castle of Culzean perches is anything but hospitable to yachts, yet the Kennedys with their attachment to the sea, their employment of the Fifes and their work in their shipyards, made the Ailsa family and their Castle uniquely important to the history of yachting.

William Fife senior designed a racing palace when he pencilled in the lines and general arrangement of the 263 ton, 113′ schooner CICELY, launched in 1902. She was the sort of yacht that Dixon Kemp had in mind when he recommended the large schooner to those to

Lord Ailsa's cutter BLOODHOUND R.Y.S., perhaps one of the most famous racing yachts ever built. (Beken of Cowes)

whom the velvet pile carpet, water colour drawings, Dresden china and a *valet de chambre* were essential, as can be seen from the photograph of her saloon.

CICELY was the first of the big schooners owned by Major Cecil Whitaker of Pylewell Park, which overlooks the western Solent, near Lymington. She was his between 1908 and 1911. He owned and raced WATERWITCH, 352 tons, and MARGHERITA, 380 tons, until the beginning of the First War.

In 1912, under the ownership of Sir James Pender, CICELY became LAMORNA. Under this fitting name and in that year she took part in the King's Cup Race, with the schooners METEOR, 400 tons, belonging to the German Emperor; WATERWITCH, 352 tons, Major Cecil Whitaker; CETONIA, 295 tons, Lord Iveagh; the ketches CARIAD II, 153 tons, Lord Dunraven and VALDORA, 106 tons, Sir William Portal.

That day was full of wind from the southwest and METEOR, with too much canvas up, careered towards CETONIA, when her master could not hold her. It was only a pause in the wind strength and some quick work with the sheets that prevented a serious accident. CARIAD II, built for such weather, won the Cup.

However, if only one racing yacht was allowed the title of Salt-Water Palace, there can be but one choice – BRITANNIA – the Kings's yacht. Her outside appearance and glorious

record have no equal. She was not only loved by her owner, the Prince of Wales, later
Edward VII, but by every sailor and longshoreman around the coasts of Britain.

BRITANNIA was built by D. & W. Henderson & Co. of Glasgow in 1893, to the design of
George Lennox Watson. He was certainly true to his epitaph – 'Justice to the line and
equity to the plummet', for she was the finest yacht, steam or sail, to come from his board.

Watson was in favour of a racing yacht riding the waves rather than ploughing through
them and BRITANNIA was conceived with this ideal in mind. Her main dimensions were
121′ 5″ overall, 87′ 8″ on the water line and 23′ 3″ beam with 15′ 1″ draught, adding up to
212 tons T.M. (1893). BRITANNIA carried 10,327 square feet of canvas. Comparing her
with today's three masted topsail schooner SIR WINSTON CHURCHILL, she would have
been 13′ 5″ smaller overall, 15′ 4″ less on the water line, 1′ 7″ narrower in beam and 0′ 5″
less draught. However, with these smaller measurements, she carried 3,217 square feet
more canvas.

BRITANNIA was of composite construction, her frames were of steel, her planking was of
American elm and the best pitch pine was used for the underwater body, with cedar for
the topsides.

The Royal Cutter was well appointed below. Her sail room, necessarily vast, took up the
whole counter. Forward of this, as was traditional, was the ladies' cabin. Then came the
companion-way, with a small sofa to port and the Prince's bathroom to starboard. A little
way forward of this was a guest stateroom and the owner's cabin on either side of the
passage way. The owner's cabin was furnished with a fine carved dressing table,
decorated with the Rose of England, the Thistle of Scotland and the Shamrock of Ireland.
Britannia herself stood out in relief on the lower corners of that piece of furniture.

The main saloon was 21′ across and was furnished with two swinging tables, one served
by an 'L' shaped sofa. The bulkheads were decorated with pictures and a plaque, dated
1892, with the signal flags of the Prince's former yacht ALINE, a schooner of 210 tons that
he owned from 1882 to 1895. Forward of the saloon were the crew's quarters, containing
the pantry, galley, captain's cabin and the fo'c'sle, which stretched right up into the bows.
During her racing days, 25 men slept and ate there.

BRITANNIA RACING AT COWES   GYBE O!

When BRITANNIA was built, nearly all yachts were steered by tiller and the Royal Cutter sported a long, white one, covered with coachwhipping, which may be seen in the National Maritime Museum. As BRITANNIA left the Clyde at the beginning of her great racing career, it would have been in the hands of Captain John Carter of Wivenhoe. He had been the sailing master of Sir Richard Sutton's GENESTA when she challenged for the America's Cup in 1885.

BRITANNIA and her crew did well in their first season, for out of 38 starts the Royal Cutter collected 20 first prizes, 10 seconds and three thirds, to a value of £1,572. Her nearest rival was Lord Dunraven's, Watson designed, VALKYRIE II, with 11 firsts, six seconds and three thirds, grossing £955.

This was certainly a fine start to a career that stretched from 1893 to 1935, in which BRITANNIA collected 231 first prizes out of 635 starts.

BRITANNIA suffered a break in her racing career from 1898 to 1913 due to the break up of the big class. This was caused by alterations in the rules engineered by the Yacht Racing Association. It was not the first or the last time that fiddling with rating or handicap has produced disastrous results and the Prince, along with many others, lost interest in the big class and BRITANNIA was sold. She changed hands over and over again. At one time she was owned by John Lawson Johnson of the Bovril Company. Sir Philip Hunloke, who became the King's sailing master, told of an aspiring owner who had almost bought BRITANNIA, but when on inspection he found that she had no funnel, he cancelled the deal.

Through all this, the Prince appeared to regret disposing of her and bought her back, only to resell the yacht a year later, in 1900, to Sir Richard Williams Bulkeley, later Commodore of the Royal Yacht Squadron. Sir Richard altered the rig, making her more snug by reducing the sail area and, therefore, more suitable for cruising. However, the Prince, now King Edward, could not forget his old yacht and she returned to him in 1901-2, to begin a new series of successes before passing, on his death, to his son, King George V.

John Irvine in his book 'The King's Britannia' tells a little story that sums up this remarkable racing career. It is necessary to picture Irvine watching BRITANNIA from another yacht with one of her old foredeck crew alongside, both staring with unblinking admiration, as the old yacht raced ahead, out beyond them:

> 'BRITANNIA was in the lead in the "Big Class", round the triangular Mouse-Oaze-Nore Thames course. The storm scud was flying over the estuary; elusive spume hissed across the short, broken, golden water; the royal racing-flag (the Prince of Wales' feathers on a red and blue ground) strained at its halyards, streaming out stiff as a board in a hardening wind. It was BRITANNIA's day – her chosen weather.
>
> 'In the far off nineties, the ancient mariner at my side had sailed as a for'ard hand in her – and in many a "crack" before that – and with a critical eye he watched the fleet round up at the mark. BRITANNIA was well in the lead. "The old lady don't want no steerin", he muttered. "Er knows the way round, I rackon – 'an how to get hoam fust as well!"'

BRITANNIA weather, though, wasn't every day and she had her quiet times, when the wind and urgency left her and the observer had time to admire that wonderful curve that swept forward from the taffrail to her bow. In these cats-paw conditions, she would move effortlessly forward with every puff of wind, her main sail sheets occasionally skimming droplets off the surface of the sea, leaving little swirls in her wake, till her crew gently handed the ropes aboard.

When King George V died in 1936, he was determined that she should not go through the indignities that followed her last release from royal ownership. BRITANNIA was not to be a monument on the Cowes green, or a training ship, as was suggested by well-meaning yachting correspondents, nor should she end her days as a collection of souvenir blocks of wood. King George loved her too much for that. John Irvine quotes Sir Philip Hunloke's words about the relationship between yacht and Royal Master: 'Aboard the BRITANNIA, the King was like a school boy home for a holiday. He loved the old yacht; he enjoyed winning, but was a splendid loser.' Her gear was sold off in aid of the National Memorial Fund to King George V and at 2 p.m. on the afternoon of July 8th, BRITANNIA was towed to her last resting place, for she was to be buried at sea. Uffa Fox saw her leave Marvin's Minerva Yard, to be taken to her last resting place in the Channel, where an explosive charge and her keel sent her to the bottom. There will never be another like her, though her lines are preserved, in half scale, in the 28 ton cutter VARUNA.

Paid Hands and the Economics of Pleasure

A good crew was an essential, whether the yacht was to be used for floating elegantly round Europe or racing in regatta after regatta. So vital was it to avoid 'mistakes' that the Secretary of the Royal Yacht Squadron kept a blacklist of yacht hands who had misbehaved themselves. This idea was abandoned in 1869 on the advice of Sir Alexander Cockburn, owner of the 115 ton schooner ZOUVE and at one time Lord Chief Justice.

The most important member of the crew, of course, was the yacht's master, captain or skipper. These three titles require a little explanation. The correct title for the paid commander of a yacht is the yacht's 'Master'. This is the proper title of a captain of a merchant vessel holding a master's ticket and used to be given to the officer appointed by the Commissioners of the Navy to be responsible for the navigating and working of a warship. The title Captain is given to a commanding officer of a naval ship and is the method of address to the officer in charge of any vessel. The word 'skipper' is a slang word of affection, or abuse, for the master of a yacht or merchantman.

'Vanderdecken' (*nom de plume* of William Cooper, 1824-1872) in his treatise 'The Yacht Sailor' published in the 60's of the last century, had clear views on those suitable to be master of a yacht. He advised an 'elderly, steady and strictly sober man' and counselled that the best place to find such a paragon was amongst the Jersey oystermen, trawlermen working the Irish Channel, Clyde or North Sea or, indeed, a West or South of Ireland Hookerman. Amongst these he was confident there would be men who were able to make 'a vessel talk'.

On many occasions, particularly with the larger yacht, the master went with the vessel. Racing skippers usually did. Such men were poached by owners willing to pay more, or with grander commands. A gentleman, of course, would not seduce another's master – he left it to his agent.

'Bagatelle', whose work is referred to earlier, was adamant that the owner should ship as master himself in the vessel's articles, 'no matter whether he knows anything about navigation or not'. The man described as master has complete control and 'has power to do what he likes with both ship and owner; though he (the paid skipper) might suffer for it afterwards in a civil action, it would not be a pleasant experience to be ordered about by one's own servant', 'Bagatelle' concludes.

Most authors writing on the management of yachts in the latter part of the 19th century recommended that pleasure vessels should be run in 'man-o-war fashion'. This particularly applied to dress and discipline, which made for a happy ship while promoting the desirable results of Marryat's maxim 'the security of the Kingdom is increased by every man being more or less a sailor'.

'Vanderdecken' was clear in his ideas on the proper rig for yacht masters and hands. The sailing master would be dressed in fine blue cloth with a rough suit for wet weather, dress cap and oilskin hat without band. 'Outward appearance', Vanderdecken held, 'has some little to do as well as mental qualifications, in commanding respect for a man placed in authority'. However, he was keen that the master's buttons should be of small size, 'there is no need of a show of buttons as big as saucers.'

When referring to the men's clothing, he had a good deal to say as well. 'For the men's clothing, you should have pilot cloth pea jackets, trowsers of the same material, and blue woollen shirts, made man-of-war fashion, with rolling collars, loose bodies, and sleeves gathered into pleats at the wrists, neat oil skin covered hats, showing the straw on the underneath part of the leaf; the light reflected from the straw gives a man's face a bright, cheerful expression; on the black silk ribands have the name of the vessel in plain shaped, moderate size, gilt letters.'

'Vanderdecken' goes on to recommend 'knitted worsted frocks' or jerseys, with the name of the yacht in crimson or white, worked on the breast. Crimson was favoured for the sailing yacht and thought less 'steamboat fashion'. Blue duck frocks or smocks, known amongst sailors by the Hindustani name of 'Doongree' with roll collars and complete with white duck trousers, were also thought right and a set of oilskins, complete with sou'-wester, were considered a good plan, for it saved the clothes and promoted warmth. 'Unless a man's bodily comfort is attended to, you cannot reasonably expect him to be cheerful and contented'.

This thought introduces the matter of discipline – 'Yacht hands will grumble at anything, but when they find it is no use, they soon turn the other way, and take a pride in carrying out the rules of the vessel' Bagot declares confidently, concluding – 'Believe me, therefore, at the root of everything, comfort, economy and safety, lies one word which has made England what she is, viz. *DISCIPLINE.*'

'The Yacht Sailor' sets out the morning harbour routine for neatness, cleanliness, order and consequently comfort and advises that the men should be out of their hammocks at an early hour.

'Let the decks be washed down the first thing, the gratings scrubbed, the bulwarks washed, the copper scoured, brasses cleaned and polished, running gear overhauled and made hand taut, ropes all coiled away in their proper places, water and coke, or other fuel got aboard, hammocks and bedding stowed away, the forecastle scoured and cleaned out, and the galley fire lit, the boats washed out and overhauled, their oars, thole pins or crutches, rudders, yokes and lines, and respective boat hooks laid ready for use.' All these duties, the author warned, should be completed by eight o'clock, by which second the burgee and ensign should be displayed. The crew may then cleanse themselves and go to breakfast.

Occasionally, when delayed in port, discipline could falter, and one or two of the crew may drink too much. Bagot had his remedy, remembering what happened one day in Gibraltar. 'As soon as I got sail on the vessel, I had the hands turned up, and made the sober ones pour buckets of water on their erring brothers, until the mixture of salt water with Gibraltar ale introduced firstly sickness, and secondly sobriety. If anyone doubts it, let him try the effects of a tumbler of sea water on the top of a glass of beer. I remember well the glorious result on the steward, who on one occasion came and told me he had seen a doctor ashore, who had ordered him to drink a wine glass of sea water every morning, before breakfast. "An excellent thing, no doubt", said I; "Mind you do". The next morning I heard a most awful and unmistakable noise, and on inquiry, found the steward had drunk, not a wine glass, but a whole tumbler of ocean wave, with, to himself, most painful results; and on being questioned as to how he liked it, the only reply to be obtained from his was: "Damn salt water! No more for me".'

The expenses of owning a yacht, sail or steam, are always assumed to be high and a yacht used to be considered a symbol of considerable affluence. Bagot, again an authority on these things and writing in the 80's of the last century, endeavours to show his readers that it was not as expensive as people imagined and that 'three or four sharing the expenses will often do a six months' pleasure trip on board for less money than it would cost if they travelled by rail and stopped at hotels'. Bagot, indeed, worked out that the expenses incurred in running a 130 ton schooner, which he estimated would cost £2,000, would be as set out below.

EXPENSES IN RUNNING A 130 TON (T.M.)
SCHOONER RIGGED YACHT IN 1880's (A.G. Bagot)

	£	s.	d.	
Captain £120 a year, or	2	10	0 per week	
Mate	1	10	0 per week	On
Boatswain	1	6	0 per week	Deck.
5 Able Seamen at 25s. a week	6	5	0 per week	
Steward	1	10	0 per week	
Assistant Steward		16	0 per week	Below.
Cook	1	10	0 per week	
Assistant Cook		16	0 per week	
Total	16	3	0	

GENERAL EXPENSES FOR A SIX MONTH CRUISE
ON A 130 TON (T.M.) SCHOONER

	£	s.	d.
Wage list	387	12	0
Additional launch man	2	8	0
Stores	100	0	0
Crew's clothes	50	0	0
Washing, say	25	0	0
Oil, coke, water	12	0	0
Insurance	60	0	0
Fitting-out	70	0	0
Reserve gear	40	0	0
Messing	120	0	0
Incidental:			
Pilotage, harbour dues, etc.	30	0	0
Total	897	0	0

NOTES:
An additional launch man means extra pay for one of the crew, with this added responsibility, at 1s 6d to 2s a week.

The Captain, mate, steward and cook will be found in food and eat in the steward's mess, while the rest fend for themselves. The steward's account for food for both saloon and steward's mess should not exceed £5 per week exclusive of wine, which depends on the taste and consumption of the owner and friends.

If this were divided amongst four friends, according to Bagot's calculations, it would cost each person £224.5s for six months, or a fraction over £1-6s-8d per day, excluding wine.

Dixon Kemp, writing of the same period, calculates that a 60 ton sailing yacht, which was about as small as a salt-water palace ever could be, unless there were other considerations, would work out this way. He is recording typical figures for a season.

Compare these expenses to those set out in the table for a typical 300 ton steam yacht – say FAIR GERALDINE of 304 tons, owned by Lord Otho FitzGerald, from 1880 to 1882. Her complement is given alongside a number of other well-known yachts of different sizes of the period.

EXPENSES IN RUNNING A 60 TON (T.M.) SAILING YACHT IN THE 1880's (Dixon Kemp)

	£	s.	d.
Repairs and renewal of hull, taking an annual average of 5 years	£70	0	0
Renewal of sails and rigging, taking an annual average of 5 years	60	0	0
Ship chandlers' stores, oil, paint, varnish, brushes, charts, flags, flags, coke, etc.	50	0	0
Hire of store	10	0	0
Sailing master, at 50s. per week	40	0	0
Mate, 16 weeks at 30s. per week	24	0	0
Four seamen 25s. a week each	80	0	0
Clothes	45	0	0
Board wages for master	8	0	0
	£387	0	0

ACTUAL WAGES PAID ON BOARD STEAM YACHTS IN THE 1880's (Dixon Kemp)

Crew	Capercailzie, 529 tons		Fair Geraldine 300 tons		Marchesa 408 tons		Eöthen 345 tons	
	£	s.	£	s.	£	s.	£	s.
Master	2	18	3	0	3	0	3	10
Mate	1	15	1	15	1	10	2	14
Second Mate	—		—		—		2	0
Boatswain	—		1	10	1	8	1	10
Coxswain	1	7	1	7	1	7	1	8
Carpenter	—		1	8	1	7	1	10
Seamen	{ 7 at 26s. / 9	2	5 at 26s. / 6	10	10 at 25s. / 12	10	7 at 26s. / 9	2
Boy	0	16	—		—		—	
Engineer	2	10	3	0	4	0	3	0
Second Engineer	2	0	2	0	3	0	2	10
Fireman	1	9	1	10	1	10	1	7
Second Fireman	1	7	1	10	1	10	1	7
Third Fireman	—		—		1	10	1	7
Steward	1	15	2	0	1	10	2	0
Second Steward	0	15	1	10	1	8	1	10
Cook	1	10	1	10	1	15	2	0
Cook's Mate	—		1	5	1	0	1	8
Total per week	27	4	29	15	38	5	38	3

GENERAL EXPENSES FOR A TYPICAL 300 TON STEAM YACHT (not FAIR GERALDINE)

	£	s.	d.
Engine room stores	50	0	0
Coal for 5000 miles steaming	140	0	0
Ship chandlers' stores	20	0	0
Repairs and renewals	300	0	0
Master, at £3 per week	48	0	0
Engineer, at £3 per week	48	0	0
Mate, at £2 10s per week	40	0	0
Second engineer, at £2 per week	32	0	0
Three stokers, at 28s per week	67	4	0
Boatswain, at 30s per week	24	0	0
Carpenter, at 30s per week	24	0	0
Three A.B.'s, at 28s per week	67	4	0
Three A.B.'s, at 25s per week	60	10	0
Clothes for master and mate	20	0	0
Clothes for engineers	20	0	0
Clothes for boatswain, seamen, and stokers	50	0	0
Board wages for officers	35	0	0
	£1045	18	0

List of Owners and Other Information

CAPERCAILZIE – Owned by John Burns, later Sir John Burns of Castle Wemyss – 1883–1891, built by Barclay & Curle, Glasgow

FAIR GERALDINE – Lord Otho FitzGerald, 1880–1882

MARCHESA (Auxiliary Steam Yacht) – 3rd Marquess of Ailsa, 1878–1880, built by Lobnitz & Co. of Renfrew

EÖTHEN – 2nd Marquess of Conyngham – 1868–1870, and Thomas Brassey, later Lord Brassey, 1871–1872

The publication of these figures did not put yachtsmen off the steam yacht, for this type of boating appealed to an expanding number. Those who were discouraged and returned to sail, later to decide to give up yachting altogether, discouraged by inconvenience, may have been brought up short by the contemporary tale of a sea going rat.

'There was a very ancient yachtsman, who had a very ancient yacht that had seen him through the prime of his days. He wanted to dispose of her, but he had likewise an ancient skipper to whom the berth was easy and the burden light. A month in the season probably saw her under way, and the remaining 11 months were spent peaceably in dock, where the old tar smoked his pipe and spun long yarns, made toy boats, wherewith he considerably increased his income among the juvenile yachtsmen of those parts, and calculated that he had secured a very peaceful refuge for the remainder of his days. The intelligence that the yacht was for sale took him all aback, but he was not to be done. Whenever any person came to look at her, he satisfied them in a plain sort of way, but when the would-be purchaser pressed the old skipper privately as to any fault beneath the surface, he would turn his quid, shake his head mysteriously, and hint that the plague of his life was a rat that had got into the mast! Then leading his visitor forward, he would set him to listen, while his grandson below, with all the aptitude of a well-educated sea-imp, by the aid of his nails and a little ventriloquial squeaking, would improvise a first-rate rat in the act of devouring the vitals of a noble spar. Rats on board at all were a serious drawback: but to go to sea with rats in the mast was more than philosophy ever dreamt of, so that the old skipper and his rat flourished and grew fat for many a long day.'

CHAPTER IV
Closer To The Water

Closest of All

The size of the infested vessel in the last chapter is not known and in this story was not important. Most yachts described in the preceding chapters have been magnificent creations and those selected for the final one were even more remarkable in both size and decoration. They were, indeed, salt-water palaces. Large dimensions by themselves, however, do not make a palace. It is more a function of the care in their conception and subsequent employment that makes a vessel worthy of such a label. Some owners have regarded, and still do regard their much smaller vessels in this light and this chapter is devoted to a few who may have held this view.

Easily the least of these was that of John MacGregor, who sailed the seas, lakes and rivers of Europe in his ROB ROY canoe. His little vessel was 14′ overall and 2′ 2″ in the beam. The paddle was 7′ long, made of spruce and weighed a little over two pounds. Unlike most canoes, she boasted sails, a lugsail and a jib. A travelling canoe of this sort cost about £15 in the 1870's and a craze for canoe cruising swept Britain at that time and was not unnoticed in Europe, for a new canoe being shown at the Paris Exhibition caused the Prince Imperial of France to join the Canoe Club.

MacGregor designed ROB ROY to carry all the necessities for a three month cruise across 'green seas, wide lakes and into wilder places'. He stowed his necessities into a little basket and into this went his cooking things, rice, soup, tea, coffee, chocolate, sugar, salt and a good supply of biscuits. He carried a spirit furnace, as he called his cooker. This, with his food basket, weighed nine pounds.

MacGregor's uniform was a grey flannel suit, supplemented by one spare pair of trousers and a wonderful woven vest, which could be worn either over everything, or under all. This was an important capacity when changing from hot paddling to cooler sailing many times a day. The suit had to be worn for months, and rubbed and scrubbed and drenched and wrung some score of times. A straw hat completed the outfit.

ROB ROY's medicine chest was a matchbox and contained, among other things, quinine for 'aguish lakes'. Then there were ship's stores in a pill-box, and the 'tailor's shop for the crew'. This consisted of one spare button and one threaded needle in a cork, guarded by a dozen pins. Everything fitted together like a hexameter verse.

John MacGregor was fond of livestock and carried a dog on some of his cruises. He recalls one of them: 'Little Rob was the best dog in the universe, light, plucky, pleasant and aqueous, not at all pretty, but admirably good.' The scholar saw him in his proper place as the 'second person singular of Cano'; and to others, ignorant even of dog Latin, he would say in plain English, 'My bark is on the wave.'

Rob's position on the canoe was just behind his master. However, MacGregor appeared to have poor luck with his ship's dogs, for one was stolen before he set off on his epic voyage across Norway and Sweden and another was even more unfortunate. He records that this dog was 'killed by a steamer at night in the Zuider Zee'.

The ROB ROY canoe could carry all the necessities for a three month cruise.
(The Rob Roy on the Baltic)

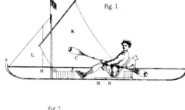

KEY

AS = Length over all 14′ 0″
AB = Stem to maximum beam 7′ 6″
C = Depth from top of deck at C 2′ 2″
　　to upper surface of keel
C,D & E,F = Dimensions of
　　　　well 2′ 8″ × 1′ 8″
K = Lugsail – yard & boom are 4′ 9″
　　　　& have an area of 15 sq.ft.
L = Jib
I = Cooking things & provisions
G = Luggage

John MacGregor lit his after-dinner cigar from a lighthouse on his way through the Swedish lakes. (The Rob Roy on the Baltic)

John MacGregor used to endeavour to obtain a bed for the night rather than sleeping under the stars or wrapped in ROB ROY's sail. He appears to have made no arrangements and trusted to luck. While paddling in Scandinavia he seems to have been without any vestige of Swedish or Norwegian.

On a typical occasion, he had put ROB ROY safe under a bank and walked through some thick bushes up to what he describes as a 'humble dwelling'. He tried to explain that he would like to stay the night but the good lady acted as though she had never seen a man in a grey flannel suit before. Two tramps were happily passing and they were enlisted, with the promise of 6d each, to explain what he wanted. MacGregor showed them the canoe and with signs, the good lady was persuaded to give him a room.

What happened after that he explains himself. 'I coolly pulled the canoe right into the bedroom, if 'bed' indeed it can be called, which was only straw, though the lady gave me a sheepskin – and a great population in it – to sleep upon, with my cork seat and mackintosh for a pillow. Madame also brought in at night some gröd (porridge) and milk, a luxury not to be had in an hotel; so all four meals today were breakfasts. One chair was in the room, and two square blocks of timber; while green bushes with leaves on adorned the walls and were sweet preserves for the mosquito game.'

A baby made sleep difficult but the inhabitants of the sheepskin were a real problem. MacGregor was not unused to their attentions it seems, for he soliloquises on tactics for the benefit of those that may be at a similar disadvantage.

'As a general maxim,' he advises, 'it is best if there be only two or three of such intruders, to let them have their way, and they will go to sleep after a good supper, and then the victim may sleep too. But with hundreds and thousands, this will not do. Put your trousers inside your stockings, tie your hankerchief over your face (making a hole for your mouth and nose), stick your hands deep into your pockets and if you can get asleep before the enemy finds his way into your entrenchment, it is well, but if one light skirmisher gets in before you are fast asleep, be sure the army is not far behind. Your defences are enfiladed and your flank is turned. You may now surrender, for the night is gone.'

On this cruise, Rob Roy MacGregor, as he was popularly known, borrowing the name from the Highland chief, arrived at Christiana (Oslo) by steamer and made his way by river and canoe east and south to the great Swedish lake of Venern, though the Göta Canal to Lake Vettern and thence by canal and fjord to the sea and Stockholm. The train took man and canoe back to Gothenburg. Then, with many adventures and taking advantage of his craft, ferries, more trains and steamers, he returned to London. In normal life, John MacGregor was a barrister. He had countless adventures, though he always managed to keep to the conventions of life in much the same way as the owner of the largest steam yacht. He is seen below, for example, lighting his after dinner cigar from a lighthouse on his way through the Swedish lakes.

After all his experiences aboard ROB ROY and after seeing the comfort provided aboard, it would seem hardly a suitable pastime for Victorian ladies, but MacGregor recommends it. He points out that it is easier to paddle than to pull two sculls in a rowing boat and 'crabs' cannot be caught in a canoe. 'The fair canoeist', Rob Roy continues, 'can always see where she is going, while she gracefully leans on a cushion, and there is ample room in the 'well' for the moderately profuse crinoline now in vogue.' There was clearly no question in his mind that she might choose a more suitable garment, for Victorians did not bend that way. After all, he had paddled thousands of miles in a grey flannel suit.

The French Canals

YTENE on the River Seine.
(Through France and Belgium)

William Moens of the Royal Victoria Yacht Club would have found all this just too uncomfortable and certainly would not have recommended anything remotely like a canoe to his ladies. He discovered, though, that the steam launch, he called it a yacht though it does not compare with others described in these pages, made an ideal way of cruising the canals of Europe. By this method, he wrote in 'Through France and Belgium', published in 1876, a party may enjoy 'the pleasure of yachting without, to many of them, the worst of all maladies, sea sickness; to say nothing of the awful fears that the slightest occurrence raises in the minds of many of our lady yachters.' His yacht, YTENE, was 72½' long, and remarkably snipey, having a beam of only 11', drawing 4' 8" of water. The engine was 20 hp nominal, and built for speed, for the boiler enabled the engine to obtain 300 revolutions a minute and so propel YTENE at 16.5 mph. Her three masts and funnel could be lowered easily to pass under bridges and the like.

His crew was modest, for he not only followed Dixon Kemp's instructions to be the titular master, but was captain and engineer in chief as well. Mr Fisher was his engineer and Mr Miller was both mate and steward. In addition, there was Allen, a 'sailor lad who cooked and did what he was told'.

The engine controls made this lack of proper crew easier as they were led to the bridge. 'This obviated', Mr Moens observed, 'all necessity for the cries of "go ahead", "stop her", "ease her", etc., which are so distressing on a yacht'.

Mr Moens described the canal scene with affection and familiarity. He was a student of architecture and what we would now describe as a conservationist. As he wandered from his yacht around a French canal town, he kept his eyes open and wrote of his feelings. 'A deep groan is drawn from my inward heart when I see the remains of some old church, perhaps Norman, perhaps of Gothic architecture, converted into a warehouse or even a brewery, and perchance hear the observation, "that you have to move with the times".' Perhaps things do not change much, though it is to be hoped his discovery about Madeira in Rouen was either not true, or was a practice now long discontinued. He describes his findings.

> 'One day, while waiting for our boat, rowing across the river to take us on board, I asked the captain of a 1,000 ton English vessel that was moored alongside the quay, what cargo he was going to take on board. To my great amusement, he said in the quietest way, "Maderira wine".
> "Ah", I replied to him, "they make a great deal here."
> "Yes sir," said he, in return, "French Madeira – the spirit distilled from the sugar beet, sweetened and bedevilled, forms the chief ingredient of this choice wine!"

Such discoveries have always sweetened a cruise too and later reminiscences relieve winter gatherings round the fire. Moens may have seen the bee barges that moved through the flowered pastures of France at that time. The bee bargee would open his hive in one location, enabling the colony to collect their nectar and pollen. In the evening he would blow his horn and the bees would come buzzing back, to be shut in and then moved gently, by barge, to new pastures. Some thought the horn was not strictly necessary and Moens would probably have wished it were so, preferring not to be disturbed by anything when yachting.

In the 1,115 miles covered before returning to the Solent, YTENE burnt 15 tons of coal,

Above
Charles Fildes, a steam devotee, used the same plant to drive his boat and a locomotive on his 200 yard, narrow gauge, railway. (Pattinson Collection, Windermere Steamboat Museum)

Above right
Two shipwrights and a 'plank on edge' cutter on the slip at Fairlie, on the Clyde. (National Trust for Scotland)

Opposite
The 27 foot, paraffin-fired, Windermere steam launch BAT *was designed by her owner Alfred Sladen and built by the famous lakeland firm of Brockbank.* BAT *was one of the first vessels to be controlled by radio, for Isaac Storey and Jack Kitchen, the inventor of the Kitchen rudder and the Lune Valley boiler, steered her round Windermere by wireless, in 1904, with only a stoker aboard. Jack Kitchen had an imaginative turn of mind and a great sense of humour. He invented a gas powered gramophone and an elliptical wheel for crossing rough terrain, which he proved by being pushed in a wheelbarrow so fitted, over his garden rockery.* BAT *is now to be seen in the Windermere Steamboat Museum.* (Beken of Cowes)

consumed 13½ gallons of lubricating oil, paid £8 6s for pilots and pilotage and 12s 3d in canal dues. YTENE was later owned by the 1st Lord Montagu of Beaulieu and was one of the first yachts kept on the Beaulieu River.

Steam launches plied other canals and populated lakes. Windermere was a favourite centre and some particularly beautiful small vessels like floating gazebos used to glide silently round the lake, to the clink of bone china as tea was being served. A particularly inventive man, Charles Fildes, was one of the first local men to have a steamboat on the lake. He went one further, though. He used the same boiler and engine on his 200 yard narrow gauge railway above the Sawrey Hotel. Charles Fildes' brother was the owner of DOLLY, a steamboat of about 1850, which sank in Ullswater during the great frost of 1895. She lay forgotten until discovered by divers in 1960. DOLLY may now be seen in the steamboat museum on Windermere.

Scotland's West

Perhaps the greatest cruising ground for the British, or for that matter any other sailor, be he near the water or comfortably insulated from it, is the West Coast of Scotland. This was recognised not only by great sailors like Lord Ailsa, but by those in much smaller yachts. The climate was roughly as today and attracted the same comment from those who recommended the virtues of the West to their fellows. The 'Governor' (John Inglis) writing in 'A Yachtsman's Holidays' in 1879, eloquently sums up the matter of weather.

'The climate of Scotland', he starts off, 'is not at all that desirable'. He points out, though, that 'those who fear showers in fine weather can be wonderfully hopeful when the weather is bad'. To the artist he indicates the 'tender tints, gloomy mist, gorgeous sunset and roaring torrents.' They are, he asserts, 'as visible as nowhere else'. One thing is certain about Scottish weather and that is that it cannot be called 'monotonous and that is a great matter; probably if the country had the climate of the Sinaitic desert, its scenery would be quite as dismal'.

CONCORDIA (A Yachtsmans Holidays)

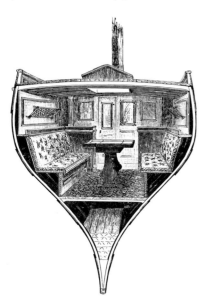

Saloon of the cutter MERMAID.
(A Yachtsmans Holidays)

However, nature has been kind and provided alongside, as dock to nettle, the proper antidote – the not unpalatable wine of the country. The method of its administration and its powers were detailed by the 'Governor'.

'"A moderate quantum about noon" – the sun being over the yard-arm. Twice its bulk of water should be added. Before dinner, it will be found to be an admirable stimulant to the appetite. It also oils the meal and assists digestion. Nor should it be neglected "between meals", as whisky rouses flagging energies and promotes the feast of reason at the evening chat, and it is the best possible nightcap. If the weather is bad, an extra nip may be found necessary and may be added to water on a hot day to relieve the danger in drinking "unsophisticated water".'

The 'Governor' gives an insight into the yacht design arguments of the time, which may well have taken up much of 'the feast of reason' and whisky at 'the evening chat'. It was the time of controversy about the merits or otherwise of beam. The narrow 'plank on edge' yacht was in vogue and was being taken to extreme by the leaders in this fashion.

The traditional faction that argued for plenty of beam, shallow draft and inside ballast were scathing about the opposite camp. The 'Governor' observed that, 'the argument is generally conducted in a manner which implies that the builder or advocate of broad vessels is a meritorious kind of person with good moral principles, a supporter of constituted authority and the Church establishment, while the fellow who would say a word for narrow boats may firstly be suspected of infidel proclivities, and is probably only restrained by the strong arm of the law from larceny and homicide. Nice distinctions are drawn between what is called "natural stability", which is a virtuous kind of stability, and "artificial" ditto, which is obtained in a mean, sneaking sort of way by lead keels, metal floors and other such iniquitous devices.'

It has taken 100 years for deep draft and beam to combine, as in the modern fin-keeled quarter or half tonner. This change arrived slowly, aided by the centreboard.

Such technical considerations obscure the really important matters, for the choice of both paid hands and guests requires more thought than almost anything else. This is particularly true on the smaller yacht, as all are cheek by jowl. The fo'c'sle bulkhead beyond whose 'green baize' the crew lived, was under an inch thick. Consider the paid hands first.

A five ton yacht of 28' and 6' 7" beam, thought in the 80's to be rather unfashionably plump, with a headroom of 4' in the main cabin, would have one paid hand. Aboard the 'Governor's' yacht ILMA, he was a 'youthful Celt, whose duties for the time were summed up in one word, "dishes".'

The 'Governor's' next yacht CONCORDIA, was a diminutive schooner that broke all Dixon Kemp's rules about reserving this rig for large and sybaritic yachts. The little clipper-bowed gem was only 34' over all, 7' 6" beam, with a headroom under the flush deck of 4' 9", except by way of the skylight, where one man might enjoy 5' 10" to dress or shave. The 'Governor' delighted in the 'greatest possible expanse of snowy deck plank'. He was not worried about bending double below as 'we didn't want to perform country dances in the saloon.'

The stately dimensions of the new yacht enabled the 'Governor' to employ a skipper and a cook. The former, Lachlan, he describes as grave and silent. 'If he ever forgot himself so far as to allow a grim smile to wrinkle his weather bronzed countenance, the momentary levity seemed to cause him great subsequent distress, and a preternatural

YUM YUM is a good example of a small steam yacht soon after the turn of the century. Such a vessel offered people with no wish to flog to windward an easier alternative, even if the desk was as exposed as on a sailing yacht.
(Steele Collection)

solemnity would overcast his visage for some time thereafter.' In spite of all this, he was a first class yacht seaman and his industry untiring.

The cook, Duncan, was mightily in awe of the skipper, who used occasionally to rate him with great vehemence in whispered Gaelic.

When the PRINCESS was purchased the crew was not increased, though the yacht, another small schooner, was twice the size of CONCORDIA. Lachlan went with his owner to the new vessel, but Duncan was away to the Mediterranean, his duties being taken by Andy, who could lace the topsail or polish the knives with equal alacrity and purpose. The only problem with the new yacht, which caused Andy much complaint, was the stove. 'It's a baad ofen, sir, a ferry baad ofen; we are trying it the other day and it is takkin' sux 'oors to bile a smaal rost, but it is never ready yet what-efer.' The owner complained that this vital information was not forthcoming ''til we were drifting slowly out of Gourock Bay on a blazing hot July day,' a classic owner's grumble.

The 'Governor' much admired his skipper, Lachlan. Occasionally the yacht master used to lay down in his bunk 'all standing', as sailors say, with his clothes wringing wet and yet seem none the worse in the morning. It could only be done by a Skyeman, for he is in his normal state when wet to the skin, the owner thought.

And so when it was time for the PRINCESS to be sold, she was replaced with MERMAID, a smart cutter of 20 tons, Lachlan was again skipper. Duncan seems to have stayed under the Mediterranean sun, so Andy was still aboard. His more menial tasks, however, were now undertaken by a third man, 'Jack', or 'Check', according to whether the command came from aft or forward.

Dixon Kemp held that a fair-sized yawl of 80 tons should have six able seamen, a master and mate – a complement of eight on deck (see Chapter IV). The 'Governor' advocated three for a 20 tonner, even though the owner and guests appeared to lend a hand occasionally. The rough guide, therefore, to be varied with rig, would be one man per 10 tons, plus an extra for yachts under 20, but with an irreducible minimum, however small the vessel, of one paid hand. On Dixon Kemp's figures of 1880, a master would require 50 shillings, a mate 30 shillings and an able seaman 25 shillings per week, plus keep while aboard and uniform, even on a five tonner.

The choice of guests was a problem that required careful thought, too, as Pepys discovered when he invited Lady Batten aboard (see Chapter 1). The 'Governor' was taken to task himself by Jim, one of his companions, when he learnt that a Dutchman was to be included amongst the guests aboard the cutter MERMAID.

'I am sure he will be an unclean fellow,' persisted Jim, 'and want to smoke in bed most likely. I will be hanged before I will occupy a cabin with a fellow who smokes in bed!'

The owner felt this was a little unkind and defended his choice.

'On the contrary' answered the Governor, 'although a Dutchman, my friend does not smoke at all. He chews not, neither does he snuff.'

Usually the first sniff of trouble comes when the guest first makes his appearance. It is not so much the 'cut of his jib', but what he has with him as luggage. This is a particular worry in small yachts and was as evident in the 80's as it is today.

When the Dutchman, a great cook, eventually arrived aboard MERMAID at the Holy Loch, Lachlan, the skipper, 'looked aghast as portmanteaus, packing cases and bundles followed each other in a stream until the decks were littered all over.'

'Pless me! but it is an aaful stuff that iss comin' aboard,' Lachlan exclaimed. Archie, in a voice soft but enough to carry, agreed. 'I am thinking we are not coin to sterf (starve) whateffer'.

Food was as important as beverage when sailing off the West Coast. It was possible that the fish trolled for and landed over the taffrail could turn out to be salmon. Andy caught just such a fish and hung it over the stern out of respect for the 'snowy white deck', but his consideration had unfortunate repercussions.

'Dinner had been arranged to come on at the unusually late hour of seven to fill up the long evening at anchor, and as we sat in the cabin awaiting its appearance, the voice of lamentation in the forecastle reached our ears. Mark Anthony over Caesar's corpse did not display his manly grief more pathetically than our provider in bewailing the mangled appearance of the salmon after having served as a fender for the punt during our run up the sound'. Such misery reminded the author of a special occasion some ninety years later.

Uffa Fox had invited the Duke of Edinburgh to dine with him in his house that had its feet in the water at Cowes. His French wife thoughtfully arranged for a salmon to be the principal attraction. When Uffa returned from racing, he found his wife and her helpers wailing that the salmon had been spoilt by the cat. Uffa, knowing that there were two fish, attempted to comfort them with a word or two of salty encouragement, but this was not to be. The grief and distress continued, if not increased, until Uffa, exasperated, picked up the remaining salmon and threw it out of the window with the words 'now you bloody well have something to cry about!'

Distress while eating under sail may be avoided by instructing the helmsman to sail easy while dinner is being served. The 'Governor' had given just such an order to Lachlan, but it did not seem to have the usual calming effect and the yacht MERMAID started to sail on her ear just as the sweet appeared. The angle became so acute that even the swinging table could not help.

'The owner had a bottle of wine upset into his plate; ketch-up permeated Peter's pudding; while Andy had a cup of scalding coffee spilt over his knees'. The explanation became obvious when the diners surrendered and came on deck. They saw that Lachlan was engaged in besting an old-fashioned cruiser of some 40 tons, which he described adversely as 'a short masted, round sided, old drogher, as weatherly as a haystack, or a Lochlomond Gabbart.' This was a fine sea-water insult to draw attention away from his unmannerly conduct at the wheel.

Loch Scavaig (A Yachtsmans Holidays)

With salmon, new potatoes properly delayed by the climate for summer enjoyment, eggs from the crofts when not sent to all-devouring Glasgow even at the end of the 19th century, and half a sheep to adorn the counter, the West had much to commend it.

There is much about food in 'The Yachtsman's Holiday' and indeed in many logs describing the ways of Victorian and Edwardian yachting. Let the 'Governor' have the last word on the subject – 'Does the reader', he asks, 'think there is a good deal in this book about eating and drinking? No faithful record of a yacht cruise is otherwise possible; there is so much time on hand, and appetites are so good, that various meals have a surpassing interest for the voyagers: if it be not so, there must be some grave defect in the digestion, or their cook is a bad one.' Be warned of the latter, for it meant half cooked dishes, uncomfortable meals, and therefore a 'southerly wind in the bread room', to use a nautical phrase for an empty stomach.

The Ocean Voyagers

The majority of Victorian owners were satisfied with the beauty and variety of the coasts of Britain, northern Europe and the Mediterranean, and did not go further afield. Yachts became increasingly more weatherly, causing a writer of the time to record that 'now-a-days ten and five ton yachts, audaciously frisk round Land's End every season in search of worthy antagonists, carrying their crews safely and speedily, with no more of discomfort than is inseparable from the dimensions.'

The craft he was talking about were racing yachts. This Corinthian spirit, the same that Lord Ailsa tried to encourage, had a following among those who cruised. A few of these intrepid sailors covered great distances. E.F. Knight was one of them and his first FALCON was only 40′ over all, small for that time. With the irreducible minimum of one paid hand, he sailed to South America in 1880 and 1881, telling of his many adventures in 'The Cruise of the FALCON'.

Captain Joshua Slocum built the famous SPRAY out of the timbers of an old boat and some odd oak trees. SPRAY was short-ended, though her sheer made this disadvantage look attractive. This American yacht was 37′ long with a beam of 14′. She would have been described as a 'real old drogher' by Captain Lachlan of MERMAID, yet SPRAY was the first yacht to carry her master round the world by himself. In 1895, the 55-year-old master mariner sailed single-handed from Boston to Gibraltar and back to Brazil. SPRAY then made her way down to the Magellan Straits, where Slocum avoided the attentions of the Araucanian Indians by sprinkling tin tacks on SPRAY's deck. This caused his visitors to wake him with cries of pain as they leapt aboard, only to spring back into the sea for relief.

He continued around the world, through the Torres Straits, across the Indian Ocean to Cape Town and New York. His adventures made SPRAY an object of considerable curiosity and reverence, which accounts for her inclusion here.

R.T. McMullen was rather different. He was driven to single-handed sailing in 1877, because he suffered from the timidity and laziness of his two paid hands. He determined to sail the 17 ton ORION alone. He disliked harbours but understood comfort, for rather than picking at food at the helm, he would sensibly 'heave to' for dinner.

However, pride of place among those who enjoyed the close proximity to the water and yet understood how to live aboard, must go to Erskine Childers. Childers had a sailor's

Amateur Navigation (Lady Brassey)

purpose, a natural love of the sea and the ability to both romance and to write about it. A short passage from 'The Riddle of the Sands' is enough to convince those furthest from the shore. Childers is describing the moment that Carruthers joined the DULCIBELLA. Davis, the owner, has already jumped aboard and is ready to receive the portmanteaus and other stores.

> "'You hand them up,' he ordered, "and I'll take them".
> 'It was a laborious task, with the one relief that it was not far to hand them – a doubtful compensation, for other reasons distantly shaping themselves. When the stack was transferred to the deck, I followed it, tripping over the flabby meat parcel which had already showed ghastly signs of disintegration under the dew. Hazily there floated through my mind my last embarkation on a yacht: my faultless attire, the trim gig and obsequious sailors. The accommodation ladder flashing with varnish and brass in the August sun, the orderly, snowy decks and basket chairs under the awning aft. What a contrast with this sordid, midnight scramble over damp meat and littered packing cases! The bitterest touch of all was a growing sense of inferiority and ignorance, which I had never before been allowed to feel in my experience of yachts.'

Childers understood the ways of a small boat. He was a member of the Royal Cruising Club, a collection of men and women dedicated to wandering under sail. Someone once described them as so wrapped in the salt-water environment that 'they picked their teeth with marlin spikes'. Over the century of years that stretch back to 1880, when the Club was founded, this collection of people have dedicated themselves particularly to making their yachts a home at sea. Some of their craft, though, are a long way from being labelled palaces and yet others may be spoken of in this way because of the endless care that is given to thinking of the proper place for both the essential and the trivial.

The 'Journal of the Royal Cruising Club' records the doings of those who cruise under sail, almost to the formation of the Club. There is now a published version, 'Roving Commissions', which comes out annually and has done so for some 18 years. This is essential reading for those who wander about 'close to the water' today.

Erskine Childers wrote a number of accounts of his own experiences in the early days of the Journal. In 1903, for example, he passed by the area that he described in 'The Riddle of the Sands', published in the very same year. He tells of 'The Cruise of the 15 ton SUNBEAM to the Baltic'. Some of his experiences in the Friesian Islands were no doubt woven into the famous story, though the 44' yawl, built in 1870, could not have been the fictional DULCIBELLA, as the former had had a draught of 6' 3", while the latter was a converted ship's boat named VIXEN. SUNBEAM may have taken her name from the famous schooner SUNBEAM, or it may have been a coincidence that Lord Runciman, who owned her after Lord Brassey and who built the second large schooner of the same name, had taught Childers to sail.

Childers records a night spent trying to shelter under that magnificent Danish cliff of Moens. Though rather different from the scene quoted before, it shows his powers of observation and of cruising in a small yacht without an auxiliary engine.

SUNBEAM was heading south when the wind came on the nose, causing a lumpy swell. As they were making little progress, they ran back a mile or two under the shelter of Moens Klint and anchored.

SUNBEAM R.Y.S. looking forward.
(Lady Brassey)

SUNBEAM R.Y.S. The Deck Saloon.
(Lady Brassey)

'A most depressing morning,' Childers writes.

'Pouring rain, glass tumbling down, nowhere to run for, an open roadstead and a gale brewing. In due course the sky cleared, the wind veered to the west, and the blow began. Our berth became a lee shore, and we weighed hurriedly in company with quite a fleet of smacks and coasters who were in the same box as ourselves. We hoped the change of wind would allow us to proceed south again, so with three reefs down, we fetched round the head and tackled the open. No use; found the wind ahead and an impossible sea. Back again and sailed slowly up and down the lee of the cliff while some terrific squalls passed over. This cliff, by the way, was the finest we had seen – a towering wall of chalk, crowned with magnificent woods, and cloven at intervals by ravines wooded to the water's edge. Finally we anchored together with all the other vessels, in a spot which promised good holding ground, well round the shoulder of the cliff and under shelter of it; a heavy ground swell running in, and we rolled horribly. At 9 p.m. the wind veered still further round to the northwest and blew a heavy gale. As we were, however, the land was still just – and only just – a protection, and we rode it out there all night, the anchor holding well, though the sea was considerable. Some of the other vessels, including a German yacht, dragged and got sail up, and shifted still further round. We kept anchor watches, and the night was a rather anxious one, but all turned out well. None of us will forget the scene that night: the little SUNBEAM plunging her bows into the short, white seas and the great pale cliffs rising above.'

To the 'Governor' aboard his MERMAID, these conditions so marvellously described may have been a little strong, for in trying to sum up yachting, he wrote nearly a quarter of a century earlier:

'Without disparaging other sports, I claim for yachting that it has all the elements of rational recreation. If a man be not too reckless in exposing himself to the vicissitudes of the weather, it has the primary recommendation of being thoroughly healthy and invigorating.'

No doubt, Erskine Childers would have agreed, after that night on his SUNBEAM R.C.C.

CHAPTER V
A View Across the Ocean

The Americans are essentially a practical people. Any search for a beginning to American yachting has to bear this in mind. In that growing country, transport and pleasure on the water became mixed. The settlers carried their experience from Europe and gleaned ideas from the Red Indian tribes who had developed a strong line of thought of their own.

The most obvious Europeans to follow were the Dutch and the British. The Dutch were unquestionably the founders of the sport and pastime of yachting. They settled New Amsterdam and no doubt used small boats as part of the economy of the colony that became New York. The beauties of Long Island Sound and the Hudson River would not have been lost on them, and the vessel that worked during the week may have been used for pleasure on Saturday.

The British had used the yacht for practical purposes too, and their settlements along the Eastern Seaboard probably adopted the same pattern of work and pleasure. The Dutch would have employed designs developed at home – wide beamed, shallow draught, Dutch fishing boats. The British would have remembered the deeper draught, but still bluff-bowed vessels that were adopted by the Water Club of the Harbour of Cork and the Cumberland Fleet. These would both have found their smaller scale counterparts in the New World.

The first craft that sailed for pleasure alone is said to have belonged to Colonel Lewis Morris. He built the sloop FANCY in 1717, fifty-eight years before the Cumberland Fleet was formed. It was only 103 years after a Dutch skipper and his crew were forced to spend a winter on Manhattan Island after their eighteen ton ship RESTLESS was burnt, so starting the colony. The Colonel, however, lived at Morrisania Manor on Long Island Sound to the northwest of Manhattan. His descendant, Gouverneur Morris helped plan the U.S. decimal coinage system and also lived at Morrisania.

George Crowninshield of Salem, Massachusetts, who was born in 1766, may claim to be America's first celebrated yachtsman. The Crowninshields were sailors first and foremost and owed their wealth to the sea and, in particular, the East Indies trade. George, in best family tradition, was sent to sea at the age of twelve and proved himself, before coming ashore to take his place of responsibility in the office. Privateering was a useful sideline in the War of 1812 and the family's brigantine profited by it, adding substantially to their fortunes.

Crowninshield's first yacht was JEFFERSON, twenty-two tons, built in 1801. He had waited thirty-four years before feeling able to own a yacht, and JEFFERSON was his pride and joy until he was fifty. It was then that he determined on a new vessel, something quite out of the ordinary. The shipowner built America's first salt-water palace in 1816, appropriately named CLEOPATRA'S BARGE. The name could hardly have been bettered, for the 190 ton brig was an admirably appointed sea-going vessel, which borrowed much from the shipowner's experience of the commercial world, but made the accommodation several times better than best. The yacht was reputed to have cost $50,000 and her ornamental interior was complemented outside by different colour schemes, port and starboard. This confusion did not prevent her from attracting attention and, indeed, visitors. CLEOPATRA'S BARGE was icebound soon after her launch and her owner continued the party by inviting everybody from Salem aboard.

He made these public inspections quite a feature of his cruises too, for according to one report 8,000 visitors went aboard when the yacht was in Barcelona. CLEOPATRA'S BARGE had left Salem in March of 1817 and reached the Azores in nineteen days. Apart from Barcelona, the voyage took in Tangier and Majorca. However, George Crowninshield did not enjoy the world of yachting for long, for he died at the end of 1817, aged 51. He had been as proud of his vessel as Charles II was of ROYAL ESCAPE.

John Stevens of Hoboken was rather a different man. He was born in 1785, nearly twenty years after Crowninshield, and played a great part in encouraging those around New York to take to the water. The inhabitants of the town were persuaded also by the lack of ferries across the Hudson River. They were used to crossing over aboard their own vessels. John Stevens owned seven yachts from 1809 to 1844, including a catamaran, DOUBLE TROUBLE, a good name on two counts, for she was not much of a success. In 1839 he graduated to the 250 ton schooner ONKAHIE. It was, however, his smaller yacht GIMCRACK, only 49' overall, that was particularly celebrated, for aboard her at five p.m. on July 30th, 1844 the New York Yacht Club was founded. GIMCRACK was anchored off The Battery, and the following gentlemen had assembled for the purpose of organising a yacht club: John C. Stevens, Hamilton Wilkes, William Edgar, John C. Jay, George L. Schuyler, Louis A. Depew, George B. Rollins, James M. Waterbury and Captain James Rogers.

The idea of the New York Yacht Club cruise was inaugurated in these first rules – 'On a motion it was resolved that the Club make a cruise to Newport, Rhode Island, under the command of the Commodore.' John C. Stevens, owner of GIMCRACK, was given that honour.

The New York Yacht Club may well have become a club of some prominence in the succeeding years with the rapid growth of the city, but their pre-eminence came from one event, the America's Cup. It was the decision of the meeting of the Royal Yacht Squadron at the Thatched House Tavern in St. James's Street, to present a cup worth £100 for the 'yachts of all nations to be sailed for under the sailing regulations of the Royal Yacht Squadron around the Isle of Wight', that brought the new organisation fully into the limelight.

The cup was, for some odd reason, known for a time in America as the Queen's Cup, while in England it was termed 'The America Cup'.

The schooner AMERICA came to Britain in the first place because of a suggestion received in a letter to George L. Schuyler, one of the founders of the Club. This proposed that an example of one of the famous New York pilot schooners should be sent to Britain on the occasion of the Great Exhibition that was to be held in the Crystal Palace in 1851. Schuyler and the two Stevens brothers and three associates formed a syndicate and commissioned George Steers, whose father had been a shipwright in England, to design and build a vessel for the purpose. There could have been no thought in anybody's mind at that time of what this new vessel might achieve. The schooner was one of the more practical items to come to Britain, though of course she was not destined for the Crystal Palace. That was filled with all manner of objects from the terra cotta works of Mrs Marsh, who had a factory in the Charlottensburg district of Berlin, to a cast iron beehive, designed by Mr W. Wilson of Berwick-on-Tweed.

AMERICA was 94' overall, 23' in the beam and drew 11'. Her hull followed the ideas embodied in George Steers' pilot boat MARY TAYLOR, named after the famous New York

nightingale. In this vessel he departed from the traditional 'cod's head and mackerel tail' in having a fine entry, and the maximum beam a little aft of midships.

AMERICA's rig followed the tradition of the pilot boats, the masks raked back 3" in the foot. The schooner was built by William H. Brown and was planked in oak with a yellow pine deck.

Her voyage across the Atlantic was domestically remarkable, judging from an account that appeared in 'Yachting' by Julius Gabe and published in London in 1902. The account came from the log of the designer's brother, James R. Steers, and is accompanied by a few trite and illuminating comments by Mr Gabe who wrote for the *Pall Mall Gazette* and *Blackwood's Magazine* and dedicated his book to Sir Thomas Lipton.

'The trip commenced on June 21st, 1851, and two days later we find it recorded that "they set the squaresail, or Big Ben, the Captain calls it," the ship making 284 knots in 24 hours, the best day's run of the voyage. On June 24th, the run was within eight miles of reaching this record, amounting to 276 miles.

'"Had for dinner today," the log reads, "a beautiful piece of beef and green peas; rice pudding for dessert. Everything set and the way she passed everything we saw was enough to surprise everybody on board." On June 26th they had "good winds, roast turkey, and brandy and water to top off with," by the aid of which they made 254 knots but on the next day the breeze was light, and the log showed only 140 knots for the twenty-four hours, in spite of which Mr Steers is moved to remark of the AMERICA: 'She is the best sea boat that ever went out of the Hook. The way we have passed every vessel we have seen must be witnessed to be believed."

'The following days show respectively 150 and 152 miles per day. The writer of the log was evidently disgusted and perchance a trifle unwell, as the entry reads: "Thick, foggy, with rain. I don't think it ever rained harder since Noah floated his Ark. Had today fried ham and eggs, boiled corn beef, smashed potatoes, with rice pudding for dessert. Should I live to get home, this will be my last sea trip".

'"Our liquor is all but gone," is the pathetic entry on July 8th, and on the following day it tells how the builder, Mr George Steers, saved them all from distress. "We had to break open one of the boxes marked rum as George had the belly-ache and all our own was consumed; but we was not a-going to starve in a market-place so we took four bottles out, and I think that it will last us". These boxes belonged to Mr John C. Stevens, Commodore of the New York Yacht Club and one of the owners of the yacht, who sailed on her in the historic race. Later on in the log he appears under the familiar sobriquet of "Johnny".

'The entire voyage to Havre was accomplished in twenty days and five hours, which must be considered remarkably good time when it is borne in mind that she was becalmed for four days (note the crossing times of the other great schooners recorded later). The second VALKYRIE's trans-Atlantic trip took twenty-nine days. The AMERICA's average running was about seven and a half knots per hour, her best record for twenty-four hours was 284 knots and her worst 33 knots.

'From her arrival at Havre, Mr Steer's narrative ceases to appear in log book form and becomes a series of observations. The chronicler expresses his opinion of Commodore Stevens with delightful candour. "I am very much dissatisfied myself with old Stevens", says Mr Steers; and here is his reason; "He has not even asked us to take a drink since he came on board, but we steal about two bottles every day. At night he sits down on the cabin floor and counts the bottles all over. When he finds any missing he calls the steward and says, "Where the hell does my liquor go?" "I don't know, sir," says the steward; "The Messrs. Steers take some when they want any." He has not said anything to either of us as yet, and if he does he will get 'beans' or something worse".'

Commodore Stevens, who was nicknamed 'Old Pig' did not appear to be too popular on board but had the right idea when it came to trying to impress the British with the merits of the New York pilot schooner. He posted a challenge of £50,000 for anyone who could beat her. Mr Steers thought this 'a staggerer', according to Gabe. It was too much, in fact, for everyone and just produced an amazed silence.

A reduction in the figure to £10,000 flushed out ALARM, but in the end the wager race was not sailed. Mr Steers recorded how she paced a number of English yachts that were racing and beat them soundly. He noted that after this, AMERICA returned to Cowes 'to get rid of the cattle'. According to Gabe, this 'elegant phrase' was a reference to some Cowes yachtsmen who had been invited aboard. Mr Steers returned home on the steamer ATLANTIC after writing this snippet and did not see the great race, which is a considerable pity for his comments would have been worth reading. *Punch*, however, recorded the result:

'Yankee Doodle had a craft,
A rather tidy clipper,
And he challenged, while they laughed,
The Britishers to whip her.
Their whole Squadron she outsped
And that on their own water;
Of all the lot she went ahead
And they came nowhere arter.'

Yankee Doodle certainly had a fine racing yacht. The American superiority in yacht design and construction was clear beyond doubt from that date. The same clever thought and ability showed through in commercial sail, too. But this was not all, for American designers had the right eye for a vessel. Their ships looked right and so wedded beauty to performance. This gift has seldom deserted American yacht designers since.

AMERICA's victory over all the British opposition was stunning, though tinged with good fortune when ARROW went aground. Her superiority was summed up by a contemporary story. Her Majesty Queen Victoria was watching the race and asked who was leading and who was second. The reply came from an American: 'Your Majesty, there ain't no second.'

It is surprising to find that after such success, AMERICA was sold to an Englishman, Sir John de Blaquiere, for $25,000 and renamed CAMILLA. He disposed of her in 1857 to Henry Montagu Upton, 2nd Viscount Templetown, a member of the Squadron, but CAMILLA R.Y.S. was neglected and she was bought in 1859 by Mr George Pitcher of Pitchers Yard at Northfleet on the Thames, where she had been laid up.

Mr Pitcher rebuilt her, giving her frames of English oak and replanking the topsides in teak. The shipwrights found that her masts were rotten at the steps and so cut feet off them. Henry Decie bought her from Pitcher in 1860 and took her back to her native shores. AMERICA was later discovered by Lt. H.S. Stevens, U.S.N. on March 13th, 1862, sunk in the St. John's River, some seventy miles above Jacksonville, Florida. Apparently she had been renamed MEMPHIS and used by Decie as a Confederate blockade runner between Europe and the Confederate States, then was scuttled. The schooner was renamed AMERICA and after the war became a training ship for the U.S. Naval Academy at Annapolis. She was one of the defenders in the America's Cup race in 1870, although then nearly twenty years old. She came fourth, way ahead of the new British challenger

CAMBRIA, who only managed tenth place. CAMBRIA was built by Ratsey of Cowes and owned by James Ashbury, a Member of Parliament and a prominent supporter of the Royal Thames Yacht Club. General F. Butler bought her from the Naval Academy and used AMERICA as his yacht. She returned to Annapolis on his death and was a strange casualty of war and neglect when the weight of winter snow brought down the shed in which she was resting in the dark days of the Second War. A replica of the AMERICA was launched on May 3rd, 1867, 116 years to the day after the original launch. Olin Stephens was responsible for her re-interpretation under the directions of Rudolph Schaefer, of Larchmont New York.

If one more story is to be told of American genius and prowess under sail, it would be of GLORIANA, for her example modified the bows of many of her contemporaries. The change was both efficient and good-looking. Owners in those days were not beyond radical boat surgery, cutting yachts in half, or bow and stern off, in order to remake the offending section to the latest idea or fad.

The thought behind GLORIANA came from the board of Nathaniel G. Herreshoff, the Wizard of Bristol, of the Herreshoff Manufacturing Company. Herreshoff and Fife had much in common, for they both knew how to fit hull line to water. Few have achieved such masterly results. Herreshoff started off designing fast sailing yachts, but in the late 70's he began to experiment with small, compound steam engines for launches. These rapidly increased in size and began to power yachts of 100' in length. In 1891 he produced this new sailing yacht for the 46' class designed for Mr Carroll. GLORIANA had a new bow, for Herreshoff had cut away the forefoot, so removing extra wetted surface from the conventional clipper shape. This produced a fine, straight line, yet preserved the classic symmetry of the clipper. The idea swept through the fleet and even the comfortable Cape Cod cat boat bowed.

The Vanderbilts

It is necessary, however, to go back a few years, to 1853, in order to celebrate the arrival of the first American steam yacht. NORTH STAR was a 270' paddler and was built by Commodore Vanderbilt. Cornelius Vanderbilt started a ferry service from Staten Island to Manhattan in the first years of the 19th century. The service gradually gained ships and routes and Captain Vanderbilt became the Commodore of the line. He began to add other methods of transport to his enterprise. Vanderbilt's yachting ambitions followed on the same line of thought as Crowninshield, for NORTH STAR was to go on a grand tour as CLEOPATRA'S BARGE had done thirty-six years before. Vanderbilt visited Cowes and Southampton before going east to southern Norway and Copenhagen. He ended his eastern progression at Kronstadt, outside St. Petersburg. NORTH STAR then made her way south to the Mediterranean, reaching as far east as Constantinople before returning to New York, via Madeira. The Commodore gave entertainments that rivalled Crownin-shield's, though he did not open the ship to the public in the same lavish way.

So started a new era of grand yachting which was to take in a rare school. This chapter concentrates on the Vanderbilts, the Morgans, the Astors and the astonishing James Gordon Bennett.

Cornelius' son, William Henry, did not seem to enjoy yachting, but he certainly increased the business and gave a good start to the next generation – Cornelius II, who didn't care for the sea either and died in 1899 – and William Kissam, who certainly did. He built the three masted topsail, screw schooner, ALVA to the designs of St. Clare Byrne, who had designed the 'Yellow Earl' NORSEMAN. ALVA was 285′ overall and 1,238 tons T.M. W.K. cruised extensively in her, but in 1892 she was sunk in collison off Martha's Vineyard and later broken up. Vanderbilt replaced her with VALIANT, 2,184 tons, again designed by Byrne and given an auxiliary rig as a brig. She was particularly well furnished below, in the manner followed by the third SEMIRAMIS, though not quite so overly ornate. The yacht was said to have been built to impress the 9th Duke of Marlborough, for Consuelo Vanderbilt was about to become his Duchess. This rumour is unlikely to be correct for the Duke was not particularly fond of yachts. Both the 6th and 7th Dukes had been members of the Squadron, the former owning the 205 ton schooner WYVERN and the latter possessing some five vessels between 1844 and his death in 1883. VALIANT was used by the British Navy during the First War and was afterwards bought by the shipowner, Lord Pirrie. She was scrapped in 1926.

The non-boating Cornelius II had a son called Cornelius III who was born in 1875. As a yachtsman, he enjoyed both sail and steam. He was almost as dedicated and versatile a seaman as his younger cousin Harold Stirling, known as Mike, who was perhaps the most celebrated of all American grand yachtsmen. But more of him later.

Cornelius III bought Lord Ashburton's 994 ton VENETIA from William Clark and named her after his great-grandfather's yacht NORTH STAR. She had gone through a few names after VENETIA, being called SYBARITE when owned by Whittaker-Wright and CHEROKEE under William Clark. VENETIA, or NORTH STAR had come from the same board as VALHALLA, for she was designed by W.C. Storey and built at the yard which was to become Vickers and grew famous as a supplier to the Royal Navy. Cornelius owned her until the First War, when she became a hospital ship. She was broken up in 1918.

Cornelius III lived most of the later part of his life aboard the fast, two funnelled, 225′ steam yacht WINCHESTER. His wife stayed ashore at Beaulieu, one of Newport's palaces. WINCHESTER was the fourth of the speedy vessels of the same name built for Peter Rouss, in 1915, by the Bath Ironworks to designs of Cox & Stevens. She could manage over 31 knots. The great authority, Erik Hoffman, tells a fine story in 'Steam Yachts' about the day that the three funnelled 137′ LITTLE SOVEREIGN was passed by the second WINCHESTER of 165′, capable of 25 knots. LITTLE SOVEREIGN's owner was the cotton king, M.C. Borden, who was 'returning to New York in LITTLE SOVEREIGN, being overhauled and passed by one of the WINCHESTERs. Turning to his Captain he said "don't stop at the yacht club landing, but continue on to Seabury's Yard so that I can order a faster yacht".'

These speedy vessels were used for commuting and had little room for comfortable cabins, as most of the hull was taken up by boilers and machinery. On the WINCHESTER IV, the owner had less than a quarter of the hull to himself. Such meagre accommodation seemed to suit the Vanderbilts, for W.K. Vanderbilt Jr., Mike's brother and Cornelius III's cousin, bought the 23 knot, 153′, two funnelled yacht TARANTULA from Colonel Harry MacCalmont who used her as tender to BANSHEE, later the Portuguese royal yacht AMELIA.

Cornelius' most beautiful yacht was ATLANTIC, a three masted schooner of 185′ overall,

137′ on the waterline, 29′ beam and 18′ draught. ATLANTIC carried 18,500 square feet of canvas. (The SIR WINSTON CHURCHILL as a comparison is 50′ smaller overall, 34′ less on the waterline, 4′ smaller in the beam and draws nearly 2′ less and carries 11,000 square feet less sail.) ATLANTIC had an auxiliary engine with a funnel in way of the foresail boom. This great schooner had been built in 1904 to the designs of William Gardner, but did not come into Vanderbilt's hands until 1924. Her most famous year was 1905 when she won the Kaiser's Cup in the Sandy Hook to the Lizard race in competition with eleven others, including Lord Brassey's SUNBEAM and Lord Crawford's VALHALLA.

Under her skipper, Charlie Barr, she broke records and achieved a day's run of 341 nautical miles, averaging nearly 14.5 knots for just under 24 hours. The Atlantic crossing of 3,013 nautical miles took 12 days, 4 hours and 1 minute.

Her sweet lines and black hull made her one of the most beautiful schooners ever built. (Author's Note: the late John Nicholson of Camper & Nicholson once said when we were discussing the hull colour for the SIR WINSTON CHURCHILL – 'Remember, black hulls never go to hell'. The schooner was painted black.)

Cornelius died at the age of 67 in 1942. William K. Jr., son of William K., the owner of ALVA, mentioned above in connection with the rapid TARANTULA, was a little like Prince Albert of Monaco and Lord Crawford in that he used his yacht ARA, an ex-Royal Navy sloop, for oceanographic purposes. He owned the Vanderbilt Marine Museum on Long Island and used the yacht to collect specimens while cruising in the western hemisphere.

William K.'s brother, Harold Stirling, known as Mike Vanderbilt, born in 1884, was the most famous of all, though he turned his attention to racing and his exploits are a little outside the scope of this book, as they came after the First War. Suffice it to say that he saw off Sir Thomas Lipton's SHAMROCK V with his ENTERPRISE in the America's Cup of 1930. He just beat the Nicholson designed ENDEAVOUR I, which was a better boat, with RAINBOW in 1934 and trounced ENDEAVOUR II, also designed by Nicholson, with the Edward Burgess and Olin Stephens designed RANGER in 1937. Mike Vanderbilt virtually lived at City Island Yard with his team during this period. It was then the hub of yachting and August Belmont, who built the 18 knot Herreshoff, and conceived and constructed the steam launch SCOUT, soon to be owned by Cornelius III as MIRAGE (1899), tried to start a yachting centre there, to rival Newport.

The Morgans

CORSAIR, 468 tons T.M., was launched in 1880, the same year as the Russian royal yacht LIVADIA. She was a very different vessel than the Czar's, for there was nothing 'turbot shaped' about the first CORSAIR. The steam yacht was originally built for C.J. Osborn and was a sister ship to STRANGER. This oddly-named vessel was of some significance to the high business world of that time, for George Osgood, who kept house in Newport, but worked, along with others, in New York, caused a sensation by breakfasting at his summer house and dining in New York, doing 15 knots on the 180′ STRANGER in between.

CORSAIR was bought by John Pierpont Morgan in 1882 and was a yacht that could readily be used for commuting from or to his house at Cragstone on the Hudson River. In the early days he knew little about yachting, but he soon learnt the ropes. By the time he built his second CORSAIR in 1890, to the designs of Beavor-Webb who also designed the British America Cup challengers GENESTA and GALATEA, he became regarded, with good

reason, as something of an authority. This was confirmed by the legendary tale, often misquoted, but taken here from Herbert E. Julyan, who took great trouble to be accurate, though he omitted some names.

Henry Clay Pierce, the oil magnate, had ordered, in 1902, an 890 ton steam yacht that was later completed for A.C. Burridge who kept her for nearly 40 years. Pierce thought it advisable to seek the advice of J.P. Morgan on the economics of yacht ownership. He asked, 'How much does it cost to run the yacht?'

'You cannot afford to run a yacht,' replied Mr Morgan.

'Why? I'm pretty warm, you know'.

'Yes,' said Mr Morgan, 'but anyone who has to ask how much it costs to run a yacht cannot afford to keep one.'

The 'pretty warm you know' is a marvellous phrase but it is usually left out.

The second CORSAIR was over 240′ long and her hull contained every comfort. Morgan kept her for eight years, the same length of time that he had retained the first CORSAIR. She would have remained longer had not the American government required the yacht as a gunboat in the Spanish-American War. CORSAIR, now U.S.S. GLOUCESTER, proved her worth by sinking two gun boats.

Morgan built a third yacht of the same name in 1899 and retained her for an astonishing 31 years. CORSAIR III's measurements were also dramatic – 270′ overall, 254′ on the water, 33′ 3″ beam and 16′ draught. This created a Thames tonnage of 1,396. Beavor-Webb was again chosen as the designer and it was fitting that her owner became Commodore of the New York Yacht Club in the same year as she was launched.

CORSAIR was frequently seen in European waters between 1902 and 1913, when J.P. Morgan died. She attended the great weeks at Cowes and Kiel. J.P. Morgan entertained royally and invited royalty aboard his yacht. It was left to his son, also J.P., known as Jack, to carry on this tradition, though the war intervened. From 1917 to 1919 CORSAIR was in the U.S. Navy, returning to Jack just before he, too, became Commodore of the New York Yacht Club. In 1929, CORSAIR was given to the U.S. Coast and Geodetic Survey, which she served until she was scrapped in 1944. Commodore Morgan ordered another CORSAIR IV in 1930 of 2,653 tons, which was over 40′ longer overall than her predecessor, but for all her magnificence she is outside the scope of this book.

All the CORSAIRs had black hulls, a distinction shared with W.K. Vanderbilt Sr.'s ALVA and VALIANT and Cornelius Vanderbilt III's ATLANTIC, and VEGLIA, built for Baron Daniel Rothschild in 1895, but later owned by G.W.C. Drexel of Philadelphia. Drexel refitted her inside and out at Camper & Nicholson and renamed the yacht ALCEDO. ALCEDO was torpedoed while serving in the First War.

The Astors

Black was certainly the 'in' colour, for 1884. The year before W.K. Vanderbilt Sr. launched ALVA, William J.J. Astor commissioned Gustav Hillman to design the 940 ton NOURMAHAL, and she too was painted black. The Astor's were taken with the name which meant 'light of the harem' and built two further large steam yachts of the same name.

The last was of 2,036 tons T.M. and was built for Vincent Astor in 1928 by Crook at a reported cost of £200,000, or just over £98 a ton – quite expensive for those days. She was well built and probably embodied the feeling of Henry Royce that 'the quality remains long after the price is forgotten'.

The yacht broker Julyan remembers the horror expressed by an old shellback he took with him to inspect NOURMAHAL refitting in Southampton. The old sailor exclaimed when he saw the white tablecloths in the Quarter Master's mess room, 'Sailors with tablecloths! What would Nelson have said'.

James Gordon Bennett Jr.

Nelson would probably have been just as surprised in casting his seaman's eye forrard if he had been aboard James Gordon Bennett's NAMOUNA. Julius Stewart's oil painting of her in Venetian waters *(frontispiece)*, completed in 1890, captures the view. There are few pictures that conjure up life aboard a large steam yacht at that time better than this one. Perhaps it is strange that the guests are forward of the deckhouse, but the shoreward

The owner's stateroom aboard ALCEDO was in the deckhouse. (John White)

The view from the quarter-deck of the steam yacht ALCEDO, ex VEGLIA R.Y.S. looking forward. The yacht was built for Baron Nathaniel de Rothschild who owned her from 1895 to 1905. This picture was taken while ALCEDO, her name under the ownership of G.W.C. Drexel of Philadelphia, was refitting at Camper & Nicholson's yard. Note the deck game board on the starboard side of the beautiful companion way.seat. The round, sea urchin cushions are of Edwardian vintage. (John White)

Right
The magnificent deck and dining saloons aboard ALCEDO. The double doors enabled both to be thrown together for receptions at such places as Newport and Cowes. (John White)

Below
ALCEDO'S study. (John White)

view may have been better, if they had cared to look. The lookout in the bows is certainly intent on his work. Ladies have never looked better at sea, or men and dogs been more solicitous to their whims. The brass, the teak bright work, the scrubbed deck, the canvas awning, and the flannel suits all fit together so well. The way the yacht is rolling to starboard as the bow rises to the swell and the attitude of the figures, gracefully bracing themselves, is so right that the viewer can almost hear the sea and smell the warm wood and sun-drenched canvas.

NAMOUNA was the first of James Gordon Bennett's steamers and came again from the board of the great steam auxiliary designer of those days – St. Clare Byrne – who designed VALIANT for W.K. Vanderbilt Sr. This screw schooner was 740 tons T.M., built of iron by Ward Stanton & Co. of Newburgh, and was 247′ overall, some 40′ shorter than the Vanderbilt yacht launched three years later.

James Gordon Bennett was a great yachtsman and a singularly proficient sailor. He had built the schooner HENRIETTA in 1861, and in 1866 he took part in, and won, the trans-Atlantic race that was organised, in winter, by Leonard Jerome, the father of Winston Churchill's mother. The stakes were reputed to be $90,000. The other schooners were FLEETWING and VESTA. HENRIETTA's time for the crossing to the Needles, on the west of the Isle of Wight, was a couple of hours under 14 days, at an average speed of over nine knots. This must be compared with the 10.4 average of the 1905 race to the Lizard, achieved by the three masted schooner ATLANTIC, nearly 40 years later.

Bennett loved sailing fast in big schooners. In 1887 he pushed DAUNTLESS to 328 nautical miles in 24 hours when racing against James Ashbury's CAMBRIA from Gaunt, Ireland to Sandy Hook. DAUNTLESS was beaten for all this, but only by an hour and 17 minutes on a course of over 3,000 miles. DAUNTLESS had a peculiar career, for she had been built as L'HIRONDELLE by Forsyth & Morgan of Mystic Bridge, Connecticut. However, in 1870 she was remodelled – her forebody was removed and rebuilt, and her waterline increased from 107′ to 116′.

But to return to James Gordon Bennett's steam yachts. Eighteen years after he first commissioned NAMOUNA, he built his ultimate vessel – LYSISTRATA – a rival to Vanderbilt's VALIANT, A.J. Drexel's MARGARITA (later SEMIRAMIS) and J.P. Morgan's third CORSAIR. This competition in yachts encouraged growth. James Gordon Bennett and, indeed, his rivals were masters at that, for they really invented the word.

LYSISTRATA was designed by G.L. Watson and built by William Denny & Son in 1900. She was 286′ overall, 21′ shorter than VALIANT and 16′ longer than CORSAIR III.

In the contract it was specified that the yacht should make 17½ knots over a run of 85 nautical miles at a displacement of 2,600 tons and with forced draft to the boilers. If this was not managed, there was to be a penalty of £200 for each tenth of a knot below the guaranteed speed and a premium of £200 for each tenth of a knot over 18 knots. Another condition, unusual in those days, was that the yacht was to be built under a roof. The quoted price was £105,000, a cost of just over £50 per Thames ton.

The accommodation for the crew was aft, which was unusual and may give a clue to why the ladies in Stewart's painting are forward, as NAMOUNA may have had the same arrangement. LYSISTRATA had an armoury and a cowhouse for two under the quarterdeck aft. The yacht's figurehead was an owl, the symbol of Athens, perhaps the best representation that could be displayed at that time. It should be remembered that

LYSISTRATA's straight stem was out of balance with her counter.
(The Steam Yachts)

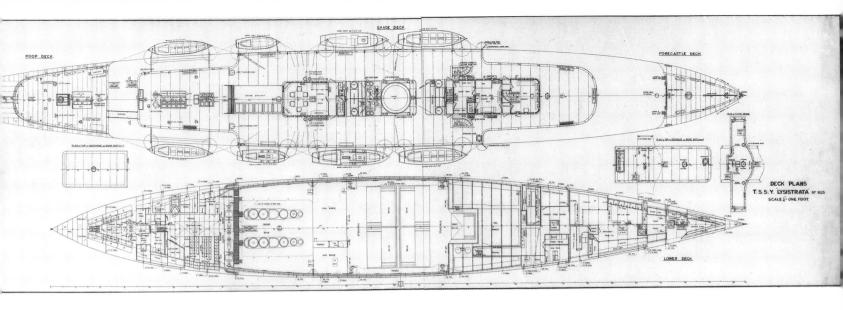

LYSISTRATA

*These two plans show the poop, shade
and forecastle deck plans with the lower
deck below. The main deck is not shown.
The crew lived aft, an unusual
arrangement for they are traditionally
housed in the forecastle. This idea works
well in Mediterranean harbours, as it
saves the owner and his guests being
disturbed by those using the passerelle or
stern gangway or suffering stares from
those on the quay. The owner had a
deck, or sea cabin, just forward of the
chart room on the shade deck. Forward
of this was the deck boudoir, with access
to the upper deck. This would have been
a pleasant retreat for guests while at sea.
LYSISTRATA carried no less than eight
boats, including three steam launches. On
the lower deck, aft of the boatswain's store,
there was a magazine for ammunition, as
the yacht carried signal cannon and no
doubt, sporting guns.* (National Maritime
Museum)

Lysistrata was an Athenian woman, and was deemed to have ended the Second Peloponnesian War. She achieved this by persuading the Athenian wives to deny their husbands sexual relations while the conflict continued.

LYSISTRATA was bought by the Imperial Russian Navy in the First War as an Arctic patrol ship and renamed YAROSLAVNA. From 1920 to 1945 she was based on Vladivostock, as a fishery protection vessel, and given the name VOROVSKY.

LYSISTRATA's most extraordinary feature, though, was her owner, James Gordon Bennett. He was born into the newspaper business, for his father the old James Gordon Bennett who had emigrated from New Mill, Banffshire in 1814 founded the *New York Herald* in 1835. The *New York Herald* published the first Wall Street financial article and the first account in an American newspaper of a love-nest murder. Father James was, therefore, one of the founders of modern American journalism. His son James was in much the same mould, and occasionally he met his match. One such time was when the *Herald* was attacking the moral and political character of William Randolph Hearst. This was being done so well that Hearst decided to retaliate and sent a reporter to dig out information about some rather seamy advertisements that were appearing in the *Herald*. The investigations were so successful that enough evidence was produced for a United States Grand Jury to indict Bennett for sending obscene matter through the post. He was fined $25,000. Bennett was furious and gave instructions that Hearst was never again to be mentioned in the *New York Herald*.

James Gordon Bennett Jr. never even mentioned to some of his staff whom he invited to meetings aboard LYSISTRATA, that they would be going off on a European cruise or to some far destination on the U.S. seaboard, but just took them with him. He died in 1914.

Closer to the Water

Another newspaper man, William Alden, an editorial writer on the *New York Times* and sometimes known as 'The funny man of the *Times*', had very different ideas. He was a follower of John MacGregor whose enthusiasm for the canoe and the flannel suit have already been described. Alden founded the New York Canoe Club in 1871, three years before Brassey's SUNBEAM was built. He was helped by Montgomery Roosevelt Schuyler, associated with the *New York World*, who became the first Commodore. William P.

Stephens in 'The Traditions and Memories of American Yachting', a collection of articles that he wrote for *Motor Boating* before 1942, puts it succinctly by ending the list of those who started the Canoe Club with the phrase 'and a half a dozen Roosevelts.'

Members of the Club imported several 'Rob Roy' and 'Nautilus' canoes from London. These little vessels, the other end of the scale from grand yachting, were used by some of the families with the great names of those days. They employed their diminutive vessels in such beautiful places as Oyster Bay and Cold Spring Harbour. The Roosevelts, the Schuylers, the Swans, the Beekmans, the Fosters and the de Forests were all canoe men.

Stephens, an enthusiastic and honoured member of the New York Canoe Club himself, records that in the 60's the journey from New York started with a horsecar to the foot of 34th Street, then a ferry was taken to Long Island City in order to catch the wood-burning locomotive to Syosset. It was necessary to drive for a few miles to Oyster Bay or Cold Spring Harbour. There was an alternative, the paddle or side wheel steamer D.R. MARTIN, that would do the journey in three hours. The yachts mentioned earlier, of course, would beat that and commuting was certainly one of their duties.

The sailing canoe in America, as in Britain, was the first seagoing expression of those who later went into larger vessels. It was a strange fact that few, if any, who made their acquaintance with the water in this way commissioned or owned a real salt-water palace, perhaps because they regarded their poor-man's yacht as that already, as suggested in Chapter IV.

Certainly, the sailing canoe habit spread across America and was going well in the Middle West.

The photograph shows the officers of the Wisconsin Canoe Association in 1893. The Commodore, G.M. Munger of Eureka, Kansas, did not follow Rob Roy MacGregor in wearing a grey flannel suit. He devised a dress of his own designed precisely for the job and sported tights and shorts.

A number of the founders of the New York Canoe Club followed the 'Corinthian Spirit' that had devotees like Lord Ailsa across the water. One of these canoeists, Billy Swan, owned the 40' sloop GLANCE while he was in college. He had read the 'Yacht Sailor' by 'Vanderdecken' and followed yachting through the pages of the British publications *The Field*, *Hunt's Yachting Magazine* and *Bell's Life*. At a meeting in the cabin of GLANCE in

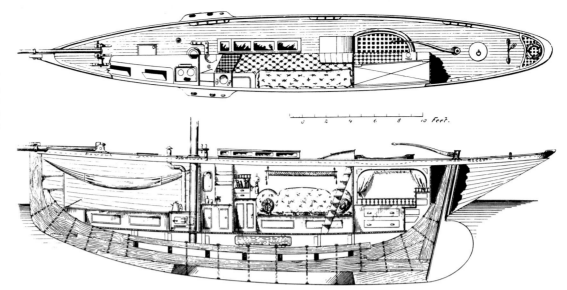

September 1871, off Hog Island, he proposed to his friends that they should form a club devoted to 'Corinthian' ideals. He spelt them out and in a few words these were personal involvement in seamanship, navigation and the management of the yacht. This included care and maintenance and embraced overhauling the rigging and doing the painting and varnishing. The name chosen for the new club was Seawanhaka, now one of the most famous in the land. Montgomery Roosevelt Schuyler, Commodore of the New York Canoe Club, was one of the founder members and was keen on the designs of C.P. Kunhardt. He was one of the 'cutter cranks'. This band of yachtsmen wedded their belief in Corinthian yachting to an enthusiasm for the narrow British cutter. The argument between beam and outside ballast is well illustrated by the 'Governor' in Chapter IV. The general arrangement of the ideal yacht is shown in the drawing of a proposed six beam cutter designed by C.P. Kunhardt in 1882. This plank on edge vessel was 42′ 6″ overall, 35′ on the waterline and had a beam of 6′ 6″. 'Six beams' means that her beam divided into her length would go six times. The yacht's Thames tonnage would have been 8.3 and her draught 6′ 6″ with eight tons of ballast, five outside and three within. Kunhardt suggested that she could carry 1,050 square feet of canvas without topsail.

Another extreme example was the seven beam cutter ILEEN, designed by John Harvey in 1882. Her dimensions were 79′ 9″ overall, 65′ 3″ on the waterline, 11′ 4″ beam and a draught of 11′, the yacht setting 4,502 square feet of canvas. Her Thames tonnage came out at 46 tons. The narrow yacht was considered more private than her beamier sister. The argument goes that there may be less room per person but they may be better separated.

The skipper aboard ILEEN was Tommy 'Dutch' Diaper, of the Itchen family from Southampton, England. W.P. Stephens recalls that when Lieutenant Henn of GALATEA was introduced to him, he did not quite catch the name. 'Was it Paddlebox , he asked, and the nickname stuck.

The interchange of ideas between America and Britain was constant and the rivalry between the two sailing nations great. The Americans had the edge over the British in sail, but when it came to comfort and grandeur the British designers and builders took the biscuit. The four yachts described in the next chapter demonstrate this artistry and craftsmanship only too clearly.

CHAPTER VI
The Pride of the Fleet

Pepys recorded in his diary for November 8th, 1660 that he had inspected the Royal Yacht MARY, accompanied by Commissioner Pett. The diarist was much impressed with the Dutch-built yacht – 'which indeed is one of the finest things that I ever saw for neatness and room in so small a vessel. Mr Pett is to make one to outdo this for the honour of his country, which I fear he will scarse better'.

Charles II and his friends demanded a high standard of comfort and decoration. Inevitably their ideas came from experience ashore. They wished to repeat their land surroundings afloat and this has been a requirement for most large yachts ever since. This means that the moment the eyes leave the deck in favour of what lies below, the emphasis should change, if possible, dramatically. The contrast was important. Above deck, nearly all fittings and fixtures were designed for a marine purpose, working in a sea environment, while below success was achieved by denying that such a rough element could exist at all so near at hand. The owner's praise was reserved for those naval architects and designers who brought the astonished guest instantly 'ashore' when he went below by creating the atmosphere of some solid, finely decorated and well-equipped country house in Wiltshire, the Dukeries or New England, well out of sight of the sea. A quiet wander through the yachts pictured here, particularly SEMIRAMIS, shows how astonishing that experience could be. Lt. William Henn certainly achieved the ideal with his Cup challenger GALATEA, as the photographs on page 55 show.

The larger the yacht the more impressive is this juxtaposition of solid comfort and watery waste. Even in vessels that spent years cruising the world, where efficiency of purpose would seem to dictate built-in furniture and no loose ornaments, this land home afloat idea continued. Erik Hoffman observes in 'The Steam Yachts' that 'SUNBEAM, a vessel normally at sea, and owned by one experienced in the movements that might be expected in a seaway, was littered with these *objets d'art*.' But the Victorians collected a mass of favourite articles around them, for they found these gave a feeling of solid security, even if the occasional expensive cascade and heart-rending noise of destruction were inevitable. After all, that age accelerated the mass souvenir trade, and the collection of mementos to remember events by. It would have been strange indeed, after all that world girdling, if Anna Brassey had not filled SUNBEAM to bursting with little solid memories of the yacht's progress.

The use of polished wood panelling aboard ships and yachts, borrowed again from the shore, became a distinctive feature. When the Swedish schooner AURORA BOREALIS was launched at Gothenburg on May 28th, 1853, *Bell's Life* records that the decorations 'partake more of the English character, and are fully adequate for any nobleman's establishment'. The correspondent goes on to describe the main cabin or saloon, 'it is superbly finished, the cabinet work being composed entirely of mahogany and varnished oak'.

Hunt's Yachting Magazine ran a series on 'Cruising Yachts and Yachting', Chapter VI coming out in November 1875. This gave advice on accommodation and decoration, favouring polished panelling. 'The selection of wood for this purpose is a matter of taste, but it is almost necessary to use a light, cheerful coloured material, and birdseye maple has become very general. This picked out with some dark wood, such as rosewood, tulip, mahogany or teak looks very pretty, but one of the most chaste cabins I ever saw was lined with all maple and a narrow stripe of gold.'

Some favoured the same wood throughout the panelling, using a dark wood, perhaps teak, mahogany or walnut, to give warmth, and relying on bright Utrecht velvets or buttoned leather on the sofas, velvet pile carpets on the floor and brass fittings, to cheer the place up. J.P. Morgan's second CORSAIR, 884 tons T.M., built in 1890, employed these thoughts to the full as can be seen on page   .

In contrast, the VICTORIA & ALBERT III whose decorator borrowed the ideas of Prince Albert, as expressed in VICTORIA & ALBERT II, adopted a simple, almost cottage approach, using such materials as pleated rosebud chintz in some of her staterooms. The use of Victorian ornate on this ship was reserved for the companion-ways and main receiving cabins. Her purpose, in these particular areas, reflected the need to provide what the guests would prefer, rather than the taste of the owner.

Sir Thomas Lipton used his yacht in an almost royal way when escorting his challengers, though he favoured the ornate approach throughout, knowing the value of such showmanship, particularly at that time.

NARCISSUS demonstrates the development of style aboard large yachts, for although she was built in 1905, the photographs show her as she was after her thorough refit in 1927. The paintwork was typical of that period and would have found no favour with the correspondent of *Hunt's Yachting Magazine*, writing 50 years before, who declared, 'painting is never satisfactory, it lasts only a short time and never looks so well as panelling, and I think it the greatest mistake to paint anything below deck in a yacht except the deck (head) itself'.

The yachts that follow represent some 50 years of interior thought, stretching from SUNBEAM in 1874 to NARCISSUS' last redecoration in 1927. They were selected because they span these important years, remembering that this book covers the period up to the First World War.

The choice is also limited by photographic material. Owners always had the outside of their vessel recorded, but seldom exposed the accommodation to the photographer's plate. The amateur photographer had to content himself with snapping the view on deck, for the light below was insufficient and meant that only the professional, with his lighting powder, had much chance of success.

These glimpses, arranged in order of date, give an idea of the scheme of decoration, the craftsmanship and the love of detail that have now left our seas. With these yachts have disappeared, with rare exceptions, the art of transforming a yacht into a real home afloat. A walk through the cabins of SUNBEAM, ERIN, SEMIRAMIS and NARCISSUS, if only with the aid of photographs, is enough evidence.

SUNBEAM

Thames Tonnage 532		*Engine Maker* Laird Bros. Birkenhead	
Length Overall 159′ 9″		*I.H.P.* 350	
Beam 27′ 6″		*Designer* St. Clare Byrne	
Draught 13′ 9″		*Builder* Bowdler Chaffer & Co., Seacombe, Birkenhead	
Rig 3 masted topsail schooner		*Date* 1874	

SUNBEAM and her voyages are celebrated, for she was one of the first yachts to sail around the world. They are well known because of the best-selling books of Lady Brassey, the wife of the owner. Anna Brassey was in the habit of recording her experiences in long letters to her father, John Allnutt. She wrote of everything that went on aboard and ashore, illustrating the account with little drawings.

Her husband was a remarkable man, too, and it is astonishing today to contemplate how he managed to achieve so much, both in politics and aboard SUNBEAM. He was born in 1836. His father had built railways all over the world and so gained parcels of interest everywhere, which acted as introductions to many people on SUNBEAM's voyages. The young Brassey entered politics at the age of 29, as Liberal M.P. for Devonport, a seat which he held for only three years before moving to Hastings, where he represented the electors for 18 years from 1868 to 1886. He carried his salt-water interests into Parliament, for he was Civil Lord of the Admiralty for four years and then Secretary for another year. Brassey was particularly interested in the Royal Naval Reserve and for all these services he was created Baron Brassey in 1886. After serving further on such bodies as the Opium Royal Commission in 1893, as Governor of Victoria, Australia from 1895 to 1900 and on the Unseaworthy Ships Commission, he was made Earl Brassey.

Throughout his political career, he took time off to cruise the world in SUNBEAM. Thomas Brassey had employed St. Clare Byrne as his designer. Byrne specialised in large auxiliaries and was later responsible for such yachts as NORSEMAN. SUNBEAM was of composite construction, teak planking on iron frames. Her success as a cruising yacht came from two prime advantages, apart from the third and perhaps the most important – her owner. The first was the successful addition of a compound steam engine and Scotch boiler to add auxiliary power to her seaworthy, easily driven hull and relatively handy rig. The second advantage was her crew, many of whom stayed with Lord Brassey for many years. The sailing master Kindred owed his name to Lord Brassey, for he was an orphan. He served aboard SUNBEAM for some 50 years, which must be nearly a record.

The crew usually numbered around 30 and Lord Brassey, who was the first yachtsman to hold a Master's Ticket, described himself as 'the Governor'. He was very much the Master, though he had a master, or a sailing master, under him, and toward the end he had both. The last man to hold the job of master was Captain Carter, the son of Captain Carter of H.M. cutter yacht BRITANNIA.

On the world voyage in 1876 to 1877 there were 32 crew, of whom 14 were able seamen, four were in the black gang, or engine room, and 11 were below decks, including stewards, cooks, a lady's maid and a nanny. On this voyage, they were accompanied by an artist and a doctor, Allnutt, their son who was 13 at the beginning of the voyage, and their three daughters. The celebrated Captain Lecky was a guest for a time and later dedicated his famous 'Wrinkles in Practical Navigation' to Lord Brassey in memory of that voyage.

SUNBEAM's principal cruises were as follows:

Mediterranean as far as Constantinople	1874-1878
Cyprus	1878
Egypt	1882
Norway	1856, 1874 & 1885 (The last with Prime Minister William Gladstone aboard.)
Holland	1858 & 1863
Round the World	1876-1877 (37,000 nautical miles)
India, Australia & the Cape	1886-1887
Calcutta	1893
Australia	1895 (To take up position as Governor of Victoria)
Kaiser's Cup Race to Sandy Hook	1905
Canada	1910
India	1914
India	1916 (To hand SUNBEAM over as a hospital ship)

Nearly overboard (Lady Brassey)

A memory of times spent aboard is best recorded in an anecdote about Lord Brassey in 'The Further Memorials of the Royal Yacht Squadron', for he was a member for 59 years, and a last word drawn from the pages of Anna Brassey.

SUNBEAM was setting her studding-sails. These were fair weather sails, set on booms, extending from the yards. They were awkward to deal with and the hands were complaining. One man said that he wished the 'old so and so' was up there himself, only to be surprised by a voice saying 'he is' and the sight of the old man himself coming out along the foot ropes.

Anna Brassey remembers a less happy occasion at the beginning of the world voyage.

> 'A new hand was steering, and just at the moment when an unusually big wave overtook us, he unfortunately allowed the vessel to broach-to a little. In a second, the sea came pouring over the stern, above Allnutt's head. The boy was nearly washed overboard, but he managed to catch hold of the rail, and with great presence of mind stuck his knees into the bulwark. Kindred our bo'sun, seeing his danger, rushed forward to save him, but was knocked down by the return wave, from which he emerged gasping. The coil of rope, on which Captain Lecky and Mabelle (the eldest daughter) was seated, was completely floated by the sea. Providentially, however, he had taken a double turn round his wrist with a reefing point, and throwing his other arm round Mabelle, held on like grim death; otherwise nothing could have saved them. She was perfectly self-possessed, and only said quietly, "hold on, Captain Lecky, hold on!", to which he replied, "all right". I asked her afterwards if she thought she was going overboard and she answered, "I did not think at all, mama, but felt sure we were gone". Captain Lecky, being accustomed to very large ships, had not in the least realised how near we were to the water in our little vessel, and was proportionately taken by surprise. All the rest of the party was drenched, with the exception of Muriel (the second daughter, later Countess De La Warr), whom Captain Brown held high above the water in his arms, and who lost no time in remarking, in the midst of the general confusion, "I'm not at all wet, I'm not." Happily, the children don't know what fear is. The maids, however, were very much frightened, as some of the sea had got down into the nursery, and the skylights had to be screwed down. Our studding-sail boom, too, broke with a loud crack when the ship broached-to and the jaws of the foreboom gave way.'

After her spell as a hospital ship and Lord Brassey's death in 1918, she was bought in 1922 by Lord Runciman who had taught Erskine Childers, author of 'The Riddle of the Sands', to sail. Brassey's executors had offered her to Pangbourne as a training ship but they refused her.

The old SUNBEAM was scrapped in 1929, after a life of 55 years. She was replaced by a new vessel of the same name. Runciman asked G.L. Watson & Co. to provide him with the vessel that Lord Brassey would have ordered if he had wished to replace the old ship. SUNBEAM II, a schooner of 661 tons, had a fine profile, was an excellent sea boat, and sailed, if anything, better than her predecessor. She is now the Greek sail training schooner EUGENE EUGENIDES.

Opposite
A view of Lord Brassey's study aboard SUNBEAM R.Y.S. *This was often the scene of discussions between Captain Squire T.S. Lecky R.N.R., the celebrated navigator and author of 'Wrinkles in Practical Navigation' and Lord Brassey, the Governor, who held a Master Ticket. Lady Brassey used to write her books on her knee. Her own desk, in the saloon, was so crowded with ornaments and mementoes that it was difficult to find a clear space.* (Beken of Cowes)

ERIN *R. Clyde Y.C., ex Aegusa, acted as tender to all the* SHAMROCKS *in Sir Thomas Lipton's attempts to 'Lift the mug' before the first war.*
(Beken of Cowes)

ERIN (ex AEGUSA)

Thames Tonnage	1242	*Engine Maker*	Scott & Co. Greenock
Length Overall	264.7	*IHP*	2,500
Beam	31.65	*Designer*	Scott & Co. Greenock
Draught	18.5	*Builder*	Scott & Co. Greenock
Rig	Screw Schooner	*Date*	1896

ERIN was launched as AEGUSA for Ignatio Florio of Palermo, though he hardly had time to enjoy her, for the yacht was sold to Sir Thomas Lipton of tea and grocery fame in 1898. Lipton took with him the yacht's master, Captain Bonomolo, who claimed to be the inventor of aluminium paint. The captain happened on the idea when in a jeweller's shop. He had gathered up a handful of aluminium filings from a jeweller's work bench when the thought came to him. This was to mix the aluminium with varnish and use it as a protective paint on one of Signor Florio's small yachts. The result was successful and so he launched the idea. It is not clear whether the observant captain made anything out of his brainwave or whether it was a story told 'under the lee of the longboat'. But to return to Sir Thomas, who was a real success.

As a young Irish boy from County Monaghan, he had emigrated to America to make his fortune, but matters did not work out that way and he returned to Glasgow with a barrel of flour and a rocking chair for his mother. There he started a small grocery business and with the aid of a good head, a singular power of organisation and a particularly smart eye for publicity, the business expanded quickly. He enlisted a cartoonist who drew pictures of topical interest and these were shown in his shop window. People from Glasgow and the West of Scotland used to make expeditions on the weekend to see the latest creations. His one shop grew to two and then into a chain, and finally a business that spread round the world, including tea plantations and large American interests. Perhaps his early days there captured his imagination and drove him towards challenging for the America's Cup. Certainly the Clyde with its ships and yachts fascinated young Lipton. The combination of the two persuaded him 'to have a shot at the old mug' himself. Lipton issued his first

Sir Thomas being given a brush before going ashore during ERIN's wartime days with the Red Cross. (Radio Times Hulton Picture Library)

Sir Thomas was very much part of ERIN's operations in the First World War. He is seen entertaining the doctors, nurses and crew on the shade deck.
(Radio Times Hulton Picture Library)

challenge through the Royal Ulster Yacht Club, Bangor, County Down in 1898. He commissioned William Fife to design the yacht. The fate of the previous Irish challenge by Lord Dunraven and his Watson designed VALKYRIEs did not dissuade him. Indeed, Thomas Lipton was asked by the Prince of Wales to heal the rift that had appeared between British and American yachtsmen after the last VALKYRIE affair (see page 80). Lipton was ideal for the task, as he was a particularly good loser and this was a necessary quality, for in the end he issued five challenges for five SHAMROCKs in the years 1899 to 1903 and 1920 and 1930, without 'lifting the mug'. Tea Tom, as he was known, achieved more for Britain than the gentle diplomacy of her ambassadors and the Foreign Office in all those years.

ERIN was very much a part of this effort, for she acted as tender for all the races before the First War. Eric Hoffman in his 'Steam Yachts' illustrates her part with a typical Lipton saga. 'ERIN's arrival in New York coincided with that of Admiral Dewey on his OLYMPIA, after his victory at Manila Bay. Lipton had sent a package of tea to each man on the OLYMPIA when she stopped at Ceylon en route to the United States, so ERIN was greeted by Dewey, the hero of the moment.' ERIN was well able to entertain the best, for below she was much in the fashion of SEMIRAMIS, a riot of Victorian ornate. It is easy to see why an invitation to a reception or dinner aboard was so valued in Cowes, the Clyde or Newport, Rhode Island. President Roosevelt was entertained aboard. Herbert E. Julyan, the famous British yacht broker of the inter-war years, remembers in 'Sixty Years of Yachts' that one evening after dinner Sir Thomas said to John Lawson Johnson, of Bovril fame and a later owner of BRITANNIA, 'Fancy me, Tommy Lipton, going downstairs to dinner with a princess on each arm'.

ERIN was an excellent sea boat with a good turn of speed, necessary qualities for a yacht that had to act as a trans-Atlantic tender. She could cruise at 15½ knots and these valuable qualities made her a useful addition to the fleet when war broke out in 1914. Just before then, Sir Thomas had received the Camper & Nicholson designed and built SHAMROCK IV. The cutter was on her way to America in convoy with ERIN when the steamboat's radio operator picked up signals between two German cruisers, announcing that war had been declared. ERIN and SHAMROCK requested instructions and the Royal Navy told them to make for Bermuda. They stayed there two or three days before making their way to New York, where SHAMROCK was laid up. ERIN was too useful and she steamed for England, where Lipton put her at the disposal of the Red Cross. Her first duty was to ferry doctors to France and then to run a similar service in the Mediterranean from Marseilles to Salonica. Sir Thomas took part himself and was decorated for his services, for he organised the despatch of units by rail to Belgrade and to important towns in Serbia. Meanwhile, his yacht continued her good service as a patrol vessel, but to his great sadness she was torpedoed in the Mediterranean with the loss of six lives.

After the war, SHAMROCK IV, or 'the ugly duckling' as she was nicknamed, competed in the interrupted America's Cup, with the now traditional result, for the America defender RESOLUTE won, sailed by Charles Adams, the United States Secretary to the Navy.

Lipton was not to be put off and tried yet again to 'lift the mug', for in 1930 he challenged with the J. class cutter SHAMROCK V, designed by Charlie Nicholson. Her tender was the steam yacht ALBION, renamed ERIN, built for Sir George Newnes, to designs of Sir William White who had been responsible for VICTORIA & ALBERT III. ALBION had been constructed by Swan Hunter in 1905 and was powered by three Parsons

Right
Another view of the deck saloon aboard
ERIN *showing the harmonium.*
(Beken of Cowes)

Below
The owner's stateroom aboard ERIN, *with*
a heavily canopied brass bed.
(Beken of Cowes)

ERIN's *duties in wartime included ferrying*
doctors from Marseilles to Salonica for
the Red Cross. She is seen here
disembarking an ambulance.
(Radio Times Hulton Picture Library)

Right
The deck saloon aboard ERIN. *A*
comfortable place to curl up with a book.
(Beken of Cowes)

ERIN's palatial saloon. ERIN was well able to entertain the best. It was easy to see why an invitation to a reception, or dinner, was so valued in Cowes, the Clyde, or Newport, Rhode Island. (Beken of Cowes)

turbines fed by two Scotch boilers. Her most distinctive feature was her single, bell-mouthed funnel, similar to the two worn by the Royal Yacht. ERIN II was broken up in 1936.

Sir Thomas was elected to the Royal Yacht Squadron in May, 1931 by acclamation 'in recognition of his great services to yacht racing'. Sadly, he died later that year, and so passed one of the most loved of British yachtsmen.

The twin screw, schooner rigged, steam yacht SEMIRAMIS R.Y.S., anchored in Cowes Roads, while in the ownership of the Marquess of Anglesey (1910-12). She is a fine example of a classic steam yacht from the board of G.L. Watson, who was never surpassed in the design of this type of vessel. (Beken of Cowes)

SEMIRAMIS
(Formerly MARGARITA, later MLADA & ALACRITY)

Thames Tonnage	1797	*Engine Maker*	Scott & Co. Greenock
Length Overall	288.1	*B.H.P.*	5,000
Beam	36.65	*Designer*	G.L. Watson
Draught	17.5	*Builder*	Scott & Co. Greenock
Rig	Twin Screw Schooner	*Date:*	1900

SEMIRAMIS was launched as MARGARITA for A.J. Drexel, a banker from Philadelphia and associate of J.P. Morgan. She was his third yacht of the same name and one of George Lennox Watson's most beautiful designs.

G.L. Watson had begun his practice in 1873, with the idea of specialising in steam yachts. However, he first made his name with the steel racing yacht VANDUARA, built for John Clark. She was described at the time as 'a delight to the eye' and 'a marvel of speed'. London papers, not given either then, or now, to using up many column inches on yachting reports, referred to her as 'the sea darling' and one paper took this sentiment further, calling her 'the steel breasted beauty'. This success influenced Watson, for he managed to retain much of the beauty, effortless ease and grace of a well-proportioned sailing ship with his steam yachts. SEMIRAMIS showed this ability at its peak. Her clipper bow was classic and the raised fo'c'sle and quarter deck, gave an excellent balance to the hull. The two, thin, tapering masts, the funnel placed just forward of the centre of the vessel and of the median point between the masts, were a delight to the eye and gave the dignity that is essential in any yacht. Compare her with LYSISTRATA, page 116, another Watson design of the same year, built for James Gordon Bennett, an experienced American yachtsman with determined ideas. The Watson hull is unmistakable and the turtle decks on the fo'c'sle and stern pick up those on SEMIRAMIS. The effect is not beautiful, for with a straight stem, the balanced look of bow and stern has gone.

Wandering through the staterooms and cabins of SEMIRAMIS must have been an unforgettable experience. Victorian ornate was at its very best and most extravagant. It was in complete contrast to the Royal Yachts VICTORIA & ALBERT II & III but these glimpses are incomplete, for they do not include the rose garden she sported until the salt-air killed the flowers.

Such a vessel required a large crew and Anthony Drexel employed over 90 to ensure smartness and every comfort. He had owned two earlier steam yachts, also called MARGARITA. The first was designed by A.H. Brown and built by Ramage & Ferguson in 1889. MARGARITA I was 703 tons T.M. and Drexel owned her from 1894 to 1899. G.L. Watson was responsible for the second and MARGARITA II was built at Lord Ailsa's Ailsa Shipbuilding Company at Troon in 1896, and was a 1,332 ton foretaste of the third MARGARITA or SEMIRAMIS described here. Drexel kept the second in tandem with the first from 1896 to 1899, before consolidating his ideas in the way illustrated. The third yacht cost £100,000 to build (£56 per Thames ton). The banker usually preferred to buy yachts and then alter them to suit. He was reported to have declined an excellent vessel on the grounds that she was so perfect he could not spend anything on her.

Drexel kept his third MARGARITA until 1911, when she was bought by the 6th Marquess of Anglesey. Charles Henry Alexander Paget was descended from the 1st Marquess, referred to earlier, who lost his leg at Waterloo. While the Earl of Uxbridge, the latter owned the famous racing cutter PEARL, 113 tons. In 1825 PEARL had survived a race against Joseph Weld's ARROW, before which Uxbridge had threatened, 'If the PEARL should be beaten, I will burn her as soon as we get back.' Uxbridge kept his yacht immaculately and on one occasion he noticed that a friend who was sailing with him had varnished boots that left tracks on the deck. Rather than upset his friend Lord Adolphus FitzClarence, or for that matter the scrubbed teak, he had a hand follow on behind, wiping the stains away as they appeared. Such smartness was the rule aboard SEMIRAMIS for the two years that 'Old Peg's' descendant owned her, making a memorable cruise to the East in 1912. The vast crew must have been a problem and in 1925 he bought a miniature edition, MAUNA LOA, motor driven and of only 66 tons, 222′ shorter than his previous yacht.

During the First War, SEMIRAMIS was fitted with a 12 pounder gun and became a flagship on the China Station. She was renamed ALACRITY. When peace came she was secured by Lt. Commander Montague Grahame-White, who used her as part of his post war charter fleet, reducing her crew to a mere 60. John Scott Hughes in his book 'Famous Yachts' refers to the Commander and his habit of buying large yachts as a 'snapper up of not inconsiderable trifles in the yachting world'. It was an apt description, for in 1924, Lloyd's lists Grahame-White as owning 17 yachts with an average tonnage of 82. By 1927, quantity was succeeded by quality and the numbers went down to eight, but the average tonnage was raised to 507, including three superb vessels, SEMIRAMIS, 1,797 tons, IANARA, (ex VANADIS, FINLANDIA & PORYVZ, while in the Russian Navy 1917-19?) and SABRINA of 513 tons, a St. Claire Byrne design of 1899, all steam yachts.

ALACRITY, ex SEMIRAMIS, was sunk on active service in the Second War.

SEMIRAMIS's saloon must have been one of
the most splendid afloat. As with the dining
saloon, most of the ornaments would have
been stowed in special wooden boxes before
the yacht left sheltered water.
(Beken of Cowes)

Right
The owner's stateroom was only marred by
the carpet. (Beken of Cowes)

Opposite
The main companion-way aboard
SEMIRAMIS was a fitting entrance to
further magnificence below. The figure
decorating the first baluster may have
been part of Anthony Drexel's doing
when he built the yacht, but more likely
was an Anglesey afterthought, for the
Paget crest is a demi-heraldic tiger sable,
maned, tufted and ducally collared
argent. (Beken of Cowes)

132

NARCISSUS R.Y.S. was one of the earlier yachts to employ the steam turbine. She was fitted with two when built in 1905. They were taken out and replaced with two Sulzer diesels in 1925. NARCISSUS is seen here, off Cowes, under their power. (John White)

NARCISSUS

Thames Tonnage 816		*Engine Maker*	Fairfield Ship & Engineering Co. Ltd. Glasgow
Length Overall 222.7		*BHP*	
Beam 27.7		*Designer*	Fairfield Ship & Engineering Co. Ltd. Glasgow
Draught 15.4		*Builder*	Fairfield Ship & Engineering Co. Ltd. Glasgow
Rig Screw Schooner		*Date*	1905

NARCISSUS came from the same designers and yard as the Spanish Royal Yacht GIRALDA, 1,664 tons T.M., built in 1894. The Fairfield Shipbuilding & Engineering Company are descended from J. Elder & Co. of Glasgow, who had been responsible for TORFRIDA, a steam yacht of 168 tons, built in 1881, owned by R.G. Duff. Fairfield also built the three LADY TORFRIDAs for Sir William Pearce, a director of the yard. NARCISSUS was better-looking than GIRALDA, for the Spanish Royal Yacht had a particularly large funnel, which, though giving her, rightly, the appearance of great power, for she could manage 22.5 knots, seemed to dominate and detract from her fine hull.

NARCISSUS was built for E. Miller Mundy of Shipley Hall, Derby who owned her until 1919. He was a member of the Royal Yacht Squadron. The yacht was one of the earliest to be powered by steam turbines, which gave her a useful operational range. NARCISSUS later found employment in the First War, when she was under the command of Captain J.P. Rolleston, R.N.R. HMS NARCISSUS II, as she was called during her war services, was armed with two 12 pounder guns. On September 7th, 1917, the armed yacht was escorting SS MANDALAY when her crew spotted a German U boat crossing the path of light from the moon. NARCISSUS open fired at 800 yards and claimed a hit on the base of the coning tower. The submarine dived but the yacht's first depth charge failed to go off. Rolleston claimed a reward, but this was disallowed by the Admiralty. Later, the submarine was thought to be U.B. 49, under the command of Captain Hans von Mellenthin, for his U boat had put into Cadiz for repairs soon after, before returning to Germany.

After the War, the yacht was sold to the Embiricos Brothers and registered in Athens. They kept her for eight years and in 1927 she was bought by Captain C. Oswald Liddell who refitted her in magnificent fashion at Camper & Nicolson's Southampton yard. This collection of photographs shows the standard of workmanship achieved by Britain's finest firm of yacht builders. Camper & Nicholson's yard at Northam, Southampton was started in 1912 and is coming to an end this year (1979), so ending 67 years on the River Itchen. The firm continues at Gosport, where it was founded in 1780, by Francis Amos who took on William Camper as an apprentice in 1809. Camper, in his turn, took on Benjamin Nicholson, the father of the great C.E. or Charlie Nicholson, in 1842, so completing a combined name that has become a byword for quality amongst yachtsmen the world over.

Captain Liddell was elected to the Royal Yacht Squadron in 1924 and was the owner of the steam yacht OSPREY, 361 T.M., built by the Ailsa Shipbuilding Company at Troon in 1902 to the designs of G.L. Watson. Liddell himself lived at Shirenewton Hall, Chepstow and cruised extensively in the yacht.

On May 29th, 1940, Dunkirk became a trap for British forces on mainland Europe and NARCISSUS, renamed GIEVE by the Admiralty, perhaps in honour of the founder of the naval tailoring firm Gieves, (now Gieves & Hawkes) at Portsmouth, was one of the larger yachts to assist in the great rescue. Captain West was the navigator and the yacht safely brought back nearly 2,000 troops. West was relieved at Dover, but as the yacht returned once more to the beaches, she struck a mine and few of her crew survived.

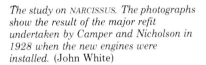

The study on NARCISSUS. The photographs show the result of the major refit undertaken by Camper and Nicholson in 1928 when the new engines were installed. (John White)

The dining saloon with the table set for ten. The peculiar pheasant ornaments were, no doubt, a reminder of the covers at Shirenewton Hall, Chepstow. (John White)

The boudoir is more modern in decoration. The treatment of the trunking is 1928 and looks uneasy with the Edwardian portrait and desk. (John White)

The saloon is classical marine, containing a piano and much enhanced by the clever use of a skylight for those relaxing on the sofa. The word settee is often employed afloat, but it is confusing, for a settee is also the name for a long, sharp, decked, lateen rigged vessel of the Mediterranean. The view through is of the lobby containing the companion-way.
(John White)

The companion-way lobby provides access both to the deck and the accommodation below. A barograph sits above a billiard cue rack for walking sticks.
(John White)

Index

Capitals indicate names of vessels, italics indicate illustrations.

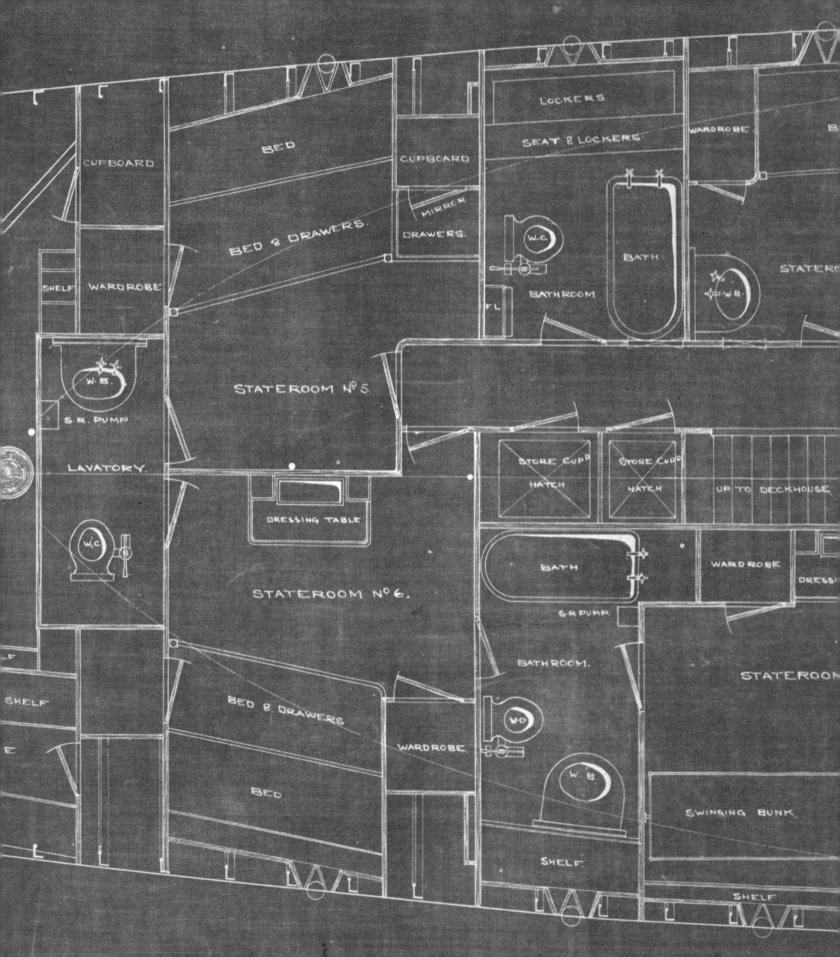